To Sue with all for Christmas

CAMBRIDGE LIBRARY CO

Books of enduring scholarly valu

May it give you inspiration!!

History

The books reissued in this series include accounts of historical events and movements by eye-witnesses and contemporaries, as well as landmark studies that assembled significant source materials or developed new historiographical methods. The series includes work in social, political and military history on a wide range of periods and regions, giving modern scholars ready access to influential publications of the past.

Suffolk and Norfolk

M.R. James (1862–1936) is probably best remembered as a writer of chilling ghost stories, but he was an outstanding scholar of medieval literature and palaeography, who served both as Provost of King's College, Cambridge, and as Director of the Fitzwilliam Museum, and many of his stories reflect his academic background. First published in 1930, this volume contains a guide to many historical places of interest in the counties of Suffolk and Norfolk. James concentrates mainly on the medieval history of these counties, weaving fascinating details of personalities and daily life with surviving examples of churches, monasteries and manors. In this tour around the two counties, the history of rich monastic foundations such as Bury St Edmunds and Norwich is discussed together with lesser-known historical sites in a clearly written and richly illustrated volume, which remains a valuable source for medieval scholars and historians.

Lots o lots lots of love

from

Badgie

Cambridge University Press has long been a pioneer in the reissuing of out-of-print titles from its own backlist, producing digital reprints of books that are still sought after by scholars and students but could not be reprinted economically using traditional technology. The Cambridge Library Collection extends this activity to a wider range of books which are still of importance to researchers and professionals, either for the source material they contain, or as landmarks in the history of their academic discipline.

Drawing from the world-renowned collections in the Cambridge University Library, and guided by the advice of experts in each subject area, Cambridge University Press is using state-of-the-art scanning machines in its own Printing House to capture the content of each book selected for inclusion. The files are processed to give a consistently clear, crisp image, and the books finished to the high quality standard for which the Press is recognised around the world. The latest print-on-demand technology ensures that the books will remain available indefinitely, and that orders for single or multiple copies can quickly be supplied.

The Cambridge Library Collection will bring back to life books of enduring scholarly value (including out-of-copyright works originally issued by other publishers) across a wide range of disciplines in the humanities and social sciences and in science and technology.

Suffolk and Norfolk

*A Perambulation of the Two Counties
with Notices of Their History and
Their Ancient Buildings*

MONTAGUE RHODES JAMES

CAMBRIDGE
UNIVERSITY PRESS

CAMBRIDGE UNIVERSITY PRESS

Cambridge, New York, Melbourne, Madrid, Cape Town, Singapore,
São Paolo, Delhi, Dubai, Tokyo, Mexico City

Published in the United States of America by Cambridge University Press, New York

www.cambridge.org
Information on this title: www.cambridge.org/9781108018067

© in this compilation Cambridge University Press 2010

This edition first published 1930
This digitally printed version 2010

ISBN 978-1-108-01806-7 Paperback

SUFFOLK AND NORFOLK

NORWICH CATHEDRAL.

SUFFOLK AND NORFOLK

A PERAMBULATION
OF THE TWO COUNTIES WITH
NOTICES OF THEIR HISTORY
AND THEIR ANCIENT BUILDINGS

by M. R. JAMES

O.M., LITT.D., F.B.A., F.S.A.

PROVOST OF ETON

Illustrated by

G. E. CHAMBERS, F.S.A.

London and Toronto

J. M. DENT AND SONS LTD.

PREFACE

IN compiling this book I have made use largely of my own notes, taken at various times during the last fifty years, and considerably supplemented for the present purpose. But I do not pretend not to have drawn upon other people's work. Guide-books, *in particular the* Little Guides, *have been most useful, and the* Transactions *of the Archæological Societies of the two counties, though these I have not consulted as much as I might have done. My debts to* Blomefield's Norfolk *and to* Clement Ingleby's Supplement *thereto are evident ; but a very special acknowledgment is due to Mr. H. R. Barker, of the Bury Museum, for his excellent gazetteer, as it may be called, of Suffolk, published at Bury in* 1907–9 *in two divisions, for* West *and* East Suffolk *; it contains photographs of every church in the county, and a succinct description of each parish. It has been invaluable to me, and often have I wished that someone in Norfolk had carried out a similar survey of that county. Other books that have helped me find mention in my text : there, too, I have tried to show my consciousness that much is wanting. Still, I believe that there are an appreciable number of facts newly recorded, and many newly brought together here. The Index is the work of Miss M. H. James.*

I have many early associations which endear these two great counties to me, and the attempt to expound some of their manifold attractions to those who live in them and those who visit them has been a very pleasant task.

Eton College,
February 1930.

M. R. JAMES.

CONTENTS

LIST OF ILLUSTRATIONS

PHOTOGRAVURE

LINE

NORFOLK

CASTLE ACRE PRIORY; WEST FRONT.

SUFFOLK AND NORFOLK

INTRODUCTORY

A HUNDRED years or so ago the number of parishes in Norfolk was reckoned as seven hundred and fifty-six, and of those in Suffolk as five hundred and twenty-three. The mere statement of these figures shows that it is impossible within the compass of a moderate volume even to name every object of interest in the two counties : I must impose strict limits upon myself, and lay down at the outset a few principles of procedure. The aim will be to call attention to the most beautiful or the most curious remains of old times, especially of mediæval times, that are to be seen, and to indulge in some explanation of them when that seems to be needed. Beauties of scenery —and these are not few—the seeing eye must find for itself ; natural history cannot be studied by the passer-by—birds and plants must be observed at leisure—so there will be no natural history, about which, after all, I am not competent to write. Fragments of the human history of the region will crop up in connexion with particular places, and a little more will be told in a few brief prefatory chapters.

The plan that seems best is to take a number of centres and group about them notes on the neighbouring places which have something— usually buildings, and among buildings churches—of special interest. I know very well how many will be the complaints of omission to which I lay myself open ; but what would my critic do if he were faced with the task of reviewing twelve hundred and seventy-nine parishes ?

I will begin by

A GLANCE AT HISTORY

The Antiquity of Man in East Anglia is the name of a very fascinating book by J. Reid Moir, issued in 1927. It tells us that in all probability there were men in this region half a million years before Christ, and it describes (among very many other interesting matters) the remains of what one may fairly call the oldest habitation built by human hands in the country, which is a wind-shelter discovered by the author in the neighbourhood of Ipswich. It tells, moreover, of what may be found on the coasts and heathlands, and unveils, so far as at this moment it can be unveiled, all the story of man and his habits and the works of his hands in these regions down to the time when the Romans came on the scene. Such a panorama is not one to be epitomized here : the interest and the actuality of it depend upon the accumulation of many minute details. My object in thus describing the book is partly to open a new source of interest to my readers, but mainly to insist on the fact that East Anglia is a very ancient district regarded from the human point of view.

When we pass into the region of written history we find the Iceni in possession of the country. We are not now allowed to derive from them the name of the Icknield Way, or the village-names of Ickworth, Ixworth, and the like. But the " British warrior queen," whom Dryden called Bouduca, our fathers Boadicea, and the best authorities Boudicca, is remembered : the date of her gallant revolt from the Romans and her death is about 60–62 A.D. The Roman occupation, which had begun before her time, continued, as we know, for some centuries after it. It has left a good many traces in East Anglia : many sites have been uncovered, many objects found in burial-places, but the results of excavations are chiefly to be sought in museums ; at two places only are important remains to be seen above-ground—at Burgh Castle in Suffolk, and at Caistor St. Edmund, near Norwich—and of these Burgh is by far the most sensational. It is probably Gariannonum (the river Yare contributing part of its name). Caistor most likely is Venta Icenorum. Of the great Roman fort at Brancaster (Branodunum) hardly anything can be seen.

Perhaps one ought to include among visible Roman memorials the roads. Peddar's Way is a pre-Roman track which was used by the Romans. Its course is rather variously described, but it ran southward from the coast—probably from Brancaster Bay, and is traceable on Roudham Heath, near Thetford, and is said to have crossed the Little Ouse, the south limit of the county, at Riddlesworth. Bits of it can be followed out in Suffolk. Of course it is most plainly to be seen on the heath or the Breckland. Of Roman roads proper one connected Caistor (by Norwich) with Colchester (Camulodunum), crossing the Waveney into Suffolk at Scole ; another is said to have

AN EAST ANGLIAN WINDMILL

run from Thetford to Caistor, though very little of it is to be seen within the county. This is the Icknield Way, which traverses Suffolk from Newmarket to Thetford. Nor must we forget the great sea wall on the west, which gives a name to Walsoken, the Walpoles, and Walton.

The visible relics of the earlier or pagan Saxon period are chiefly confined to the objects which have been dug up in cemeteries and relegated to museums. From the seventh century onwards East Anglia was Christian, as will be told in more detail in another chapter. Here the reader shall be reminded that fairly early in the seventh century (630) a bishopric was set up at Dunwich in Suffolk, and later (673) another at Elmham. The evidence is strong that this Elmham was North Elmham in Norfolk ; but there is a group of South Elmhams in Suffolk, and in spite of the recent uncovering of the site of an important church at North Elmham, there are still champions of Suffolk who hold to the theory of Harrod the antiquary, and vote for the " Old Minster " at South Elmham St. Cross.

Another Church institution is connected with Suffolk. It is held by a group of investigators that the Councils of Clovesho, which in 673 were appointed to take place annually, and were in fact held, how regularly we do not know, until 825, met at a spot where four ways join in the parish of Mildenhall and hamlet of West Row. Among these Councils those of 747 (which promulgated some thirty decrees regulating the conduct of bishops) and 823 (in which the integrity of the See of Canterbury was restored) were highly important. Former historians have located Clovesho at such various places as Cliffe-at-Hoo (Kent), Abingdon, Tewkesbury, Hertford, and " near London." I do not know how far the Suffolk identification, first made about forty years ago, is accepted ; but clearly it is worth mentioning.

The Danish invasion of 866 extinguished both the bishoprics, and apparently laid waste every monastery and parish church in the two counties. Of Dunwich we hear no more after this catastrophe ; but Elmham was re-established about 960, and at the same time there was a tremendous activity in rebuilding the parish churches, and several of the abbeys, e.g. St. Benet's Hulme, were revived. The result is that in Domesday well over three hundred churches are mentioned in each county. Mr. William Page, in a very interesting article in *Archæologia* (Vol. 66), has dwelt on the " peculiar character of the development of the parish church in these districts." Elsewhere in England the churches had been " apparently built and held by thegns and large landowners, but in East Anglia they were frequently on the lands of groups of freemen and others, by whom, or their predecessors, they were probably built and endowed." He

KERSEY, SUFFOLK. PART OF SCREEN

goes on to give instances of this " communal action in the building of churches " which is not found in any other part of England.

Of the buildings thus set up few indeed retain any distinguishable portions of their original structure. Yet it is held by good authorities that some of the round towers which are so common (there are 125 in Norfolk and 42 in Suffolk) go back to the tenth century.

What the Normans have left we shall notice from time to time in our survey.

A local immigration of the early fourteenth century which had important consequences was that of Flemish weavers, which had begun already in the twelfth century. To their activities we owe indirectly the multitude of large and fine churches ; for the sheep-farming trade fed the woollen trade, and made Norfolk especially rich ; Suffolk also had its share. Worstead in Norfolk and Kersey and Lindsey in Suffolk (*pace* the *Oxford Dictionary*) have given their names to well-known fabrics.

The size of these village churches, built out of the profits of wool or weaving, is a standing puzzle to those who " nicely calculating less or more " cannot imagine why, when only 150 " sittings " were needed, space for a thousand people should have been provided. They inquire whether the population was not much larger in old times than now. Perhaps it was larger, but it was not the population that dictated the size of the church, but higher motives of thankfulness and of devotion. If every now and then a little flavour of ostentation crept in—a hankering to have a better and bigger church than our neighbours a mile off—we can find it in our hearts to forgive that.

Not even the most superficial glance at the history—and the present one is as sketchy as can be—can pass over the great cataclysm of the Black Death, which was at its worst in the summer of 1349. Dr. Jessopp has collected the statistics of the mortality among the clergy, and the figures that apply to that one class would have to be multiplied we know not how often for the general population. Two thousand clergy, he guesses, perished in a few months in the diocese ; certainly 800 parishes lost their incumbents, and of the religious houses some were totally emptied, and all suffered terribly. The dislocation of social life is written all over the history of England ; the effect on public works and on the arts was paralysing. But hardly less surprising than the catastrophe was the recovery of prosperity. The sumptuous churches of which I have been speaking belong to a period later than the Black Death.

I need not carry on my survey in chronicle-fashion : I have touched on the way in which the churches came to be where they are. I will now add a few pages on what is to be seen outside and inside them.

The Perpendicular style which seems to have taken shape in the western side of England in the fourteenth century (Gloucester Cathedral shows Perpendicular work of about 1336) made its way all over England, dominated the fifteenth century, and preponderates in the churches of East Anglia. Few indeed are those which do not show remodelling, more or less extensive, in this style. The Norman doorways will be left, perhaps, and the thirteenth- or fourteenth-century arcading between nave and aisles ; but very commonly a clerestory will have been added, a tower rebuilt or heightened, and chantries annexed ; and almost always small old windows will have been replaced by larger ones, which not only admit more light, but afford more opportunity for the display of painted glass.

Characteristic of East Anglian churches is the use of flint : plain flint, knapped smooth, forms the beautiful surfaces of many towers and walls, and flint and stone panelling adorns the bases of towers and porches and runs along below the battlements of aisles. The stone is panelled with pieces of smooth flint set in shallow hollows, so that the letters of an inscription or

LAVENHAM TOWER, SUFFOLK

monogram, or heraldic devices appear as it were on a ground of dark flint. This " flush work " is very beautiful in effect.

Inside the churches the timber roofs are often a magnificent feature,

especially those which show a row of angels with spread wings on
the ends of the projecting beams called hammer-beams ; occasionally
there is even a double hammer-beam roof with four rows of angels.
On the supports called helves, which stand on brackets between the
clerestory windows, there should be a series of saint-figures.

Then there is a good deal of furniture in the way of seating and
screens. Special books on these have been written in recent years,
and admirably illustrated. The bench-ends are worked into what
used to be called poppy-heads—the older name was popeys ; these
have figures of angels, men, birds, and beasts in the round, which are
worth noting. The screens, few of which are earlier than 1400,
and many as late as 1500, have usually had their lower panels painted
with figures of saints, which are rarely of great artistic merit, but
help us to get some idea of the popular devotion of the late fifteenth
and early sixteenth centuries. These paintings are most plentiful in
Norfolk ; Suffolk also has good specimens ; in the rest of England
they are almost confined to Devonshire.

There are wall-paintings in good numbers : faint and ill-preserved
for the most part, but always to be looked at. Not many of those that
survive in these counties are as old as the thirteenth century, which
is regrettable, because the paintings of that period usually tell some
Bible story or the life of a saint, whereas the later ones are rather
" votive " than narrative. St. Christopher (seventy-two of these),
St. George, the Seven Works of Mercy, the Three Dead and Three
Living, the Last Judgment, occur over and over again.

The aggregate amount of old glass is large, but scattered and fragmentary. Few whole windows have survived : I do not indeed
recollect one that is in its original condition ; but there are multitudes
of small figures in the tracery-lights of windows, much canopy-work,
not a few storied panels, and many cases where whole windows have
been filled with fragments brought together from every part of the
church : a mistaken procedure. There is also a quantity of foreign
glass of the sixteenth and later centuries, imported in the early years
of the nineteenth century, purchased by enlightened squires, and
placed in the parish churches. Some of this is of excellent quality.

Brasses have been most plentiful, and the finest in England are to
be found here ; but the brass-rubber knows this well. He is catered
for in many an easily accessible manual. I shall not dwell much

therefore upon brasses in this book. The more stately sepulchres of stone will receive occasional notice.

Rich as the churches are—taking them all round—they have lost enormously even since the Civil Wars. In that period destruction was official and methodical. We have a portion of a Journal of William Dowsing, a commissioner under the Earl of Manchester, which records his doings in about 150 places in Suffolk in 1643-4. But the casualties suffered in the eighteenth century at the hands of sometimes well-meaning but more often negligent and always stupid persons in charge are almost more distressing because purposeless. One can judge of them by such a book as Blomefield's *History of Norfolk :* he died in 1752. I have filled a sizeable note-book with the particulars of stained-glass and imagery which he happens to notice (and he is not systematic in this matter). Entire windows described by him are absolutely gone, and very many which were fragmentary in his time are complete blanks.

Nineteenth- (and twentieth-) century restorers deserve almost harder words than eighteenth-

BARDWELL, SUFFOLK. FIGURE OF SIR WILLIAM BARDWELL IN WINDOW OF NAVE

century churchwardens, for they have sinned against light ; at least they have not chosen to seek the light they might have had.   I am thinking more of the architects and builders than of the worthy persons who gave of their abundance or their penury to beautify their village church.   Among the many sins which came to be committed in the restoration process, two which are not yet extinct are particularly grievous and hard to forgive : the addition of organ-chambers and the introduction of varnished pitch-pine ; a third, perhaps most hateful of all, is the filling of the windows with what is called (Heaven knows why !) cathedral glass.   The pictured glass is often bad enough in all con-science ; but to substitute for good old clear glazing, through which the waving trees might be seen, this tinted outrage, which would disgrace the refreshment-room of the meanest of railway stations, is so foolish that no polite language can reach it.

SAINTS AND SHRINES

EAST Anglia, like every other district of England, has its own group of saints, great and little, and also its own centres of popular worship, to which resort was made either because the body of some holy person lay there or because it was the repository of some famous relic : the two reasons are not quite identical.

In the following pages I will discuss first the saints and their shrines, and then the relics and theirs.

The Christianity of East Anglia (by which term I intend Norfolk and Suffolk to be understood) began in the seventh century.   If there were Roman Christians or British Christians in that region before the coming of the English, I believe they have left no trace.

Bede, as usual, is our primary authority.   As is the wont of early chroniclers, he hangs his information upon the succession of the kings, or, where there were any, the bishops of his districts.   The kings of East Anglia were of a line called the Uffingas, the descendants of Uffa.   The third of them was Redwald.   In his youth Redwald became a Christian, in Kent, but returning to his own kingdom he apostatized under the influence of his queen and " certain false teachers," or partly apostatized, for he is said to have kept two altars in his chapel or temple, one (the smaller) heathen, the other Christian. Where this hybrid worship went on is not recorded : it may have been at Rendlesham, in Suffolk (which was the site of a palace), for in 1687 a silver crown, reputed to have been Redwald's, was dug up, and (it is painful to relate) was melted down almost at once, so that we know nothing of its quality. Redwald seems to have died about 617. His son Eorpwald succeeded, and was persuaded by Edwin, king of Northumbria, to become a Christian not long before his death : he was murdered in 628.

A stepson of Redwald's, Sigebert, now comes on the scene. During Eorpwald's life he had been exiled in France, and there became a most devout Christian, and on his accession determined that his subjects should adopt the faith. To him, authorized by Honorius, Archbishop of Canterbury, came Felix, a Burgundian, who ranks as the Apostle of East Anglia. Sigebert had, we are told, learned to know him in France. Felix was the first bishop of East Anglia, his See being fixed at a place which Bede calls Donmoc : we may safely identify it with Dunwich. These two, the king Sigebert whose feast is on January 25 and the bishop Felix commemorated on March 8, are the first East Anglian saints. Of Sigebert it remains to be told that after associating his kinsman Egric with him as joint king, he retired into a monastery founded by himself, it is said, at Beaduricesworth—afterwards known as Bury—and that in or about 635, when the heathen Penda king of Mercia attacked his land, he was brought out, against his will, to oppose the invaders. He went with the host, but unarmed, carrying only a wand, and both he and Egric fell in battle. So he ranks as a martyr. But his memory faded, and I know of no trace of later mediæval devotion, no sanctuary or image that recalled him to the eye or mind.

Felix, whose missionary work Bede says was very fruitful, also failed to impress himself on the imagination of later generations. Nor did his body rest in the scene of his labours : from Soham in Cambridgeshire, where he died, it was taken to Ramsey Abbey. A wall-painting of a bishop at Soham probably represents him. In Suffolk a church was dedicated to him at Walton, near Felixstowe, but we are told that neither Felixstowe nor Flixton can have been named after him. Another memorial of him, however, survived almost to our own times, and perhaps may be lurking somewhere even now. In Henry VIII's time the monks of the small priory of Eye possessed the Gospel book of St. Felix, brought from Dunwich, which Leland saw there. It was written, he says, in Lombardic characters, by which he means some large unfamiliar script. From the monks the book passed to the Corporation of Eye, and was known as the Red Book of Eye ; upon it oaths were taken. It is mentioned in the town records in the eighteenth, if not the nineteenth, century. It is not now to be found. A good many years ago Dr. G. F. Maclear, who had been employed in inspecting the records at Eye, told me that it was there reported that the Red Book had been sent for to the neighbouring mansion of Brome Hall, and had there (*proh nefas !*) been cut up for game-labels—a harrowing and, I hope, not very certain story. My own inquiries at Brome Hall showed that nothing was known there. I cherish the hope that remnants of the book may still exist in some deed-box.

We must not leave Sigebert's reign without mention of another of his helpers in the evangelization of the kingdom. I mean the Irishman St. Fursey, who came with several compatriots, Foillan (his own brother), Gobban, Dicuil, into Suffolk, and after some time spent in teaching, retired to monastic life on an estate given him by Sigebert. He built a monastery at Cnobberesburch, adapting to his purpose, it seems, some part of the Roman fort at Burgh Castle. Here it was that he saw the remarkable vision of heaven and hell which is given in full in his *Life* and is quoted in part by Bede ; and hence it was that he crossed to France, leaving Foillan in command, and founded a more famous monastery at Lagny, near Paris. Foillan and the others eventually followed him, and all have their shrines in North-eastern France : that of Fursey is at Péronne.

The next king of the East Angles was also a saint and martyr, Anna, nephew of Redwald and father of at least five sainted persons— four women and a man. The women were Etheldreda (of Ely), Ethelburga (of Faremoutier, in France), Sexburga queen of Kent, and Withburga of East Dereham ; the man was Jurmin, of whom more anon. Anna, like Sigebert, fell in battle fighting against the old heathen Penda, in 654, after a reign of nineteen years. This happened in the neighbourhood of Blythburgh : a plain tomb of later date in the church there was long pointed out as Anna's, but without probability. In that same battle Jurmin also fell. His name is often miswritten as Germanus or Firminus : his body did rest at Blythburgh for a long time. In the eleventh century it was appropriated, no doubt to the disgust of the Blythburgh people, by the masterful convent of Bury, and there, at or near the Chapel of the Virgin in the central eastern apse of the Abbey church (as I think) a handsome silver shrine contained it until the Dissolution. No very special cult attached to it that I can discover. The shrine figured in the great processions : the commemorations were on February 23 and May 31.

Coupled with Jurmin on May 31 in Bury Calendars is Botolph, and his relics for a time rested beside Jurmin, though later there was a separate chapel of St. Botolph which contained either all his relics or possibly only his arm. It has been the habit of those who have noticed the Bury St. Botolph at all to view him as an obscure bishop, distinct from the Abbot of Ikanhoe, to whom between sixty and seventy churches are dedicated, and who is the eponymous patron of Boston. But a recent writer, Mr. Stevenson, in the *Proceedings of the Suffolk Institute of Archæology* (1922), has made a very good case for believing that the Bury saint was both bishop (without a see) and abbot, and is identical with the more famous Botolph, and that his monastery at Ikanhoe was really at Iken, that very attractive secluded spot on the River Alde. Botolph, or Botwulf, is said by one old authority to have been of Irish birth : he must have died about 680—his principal day in the Calendar is June 17.

We will turn for a moment to Anna's other children. Etheldreda, Ethelburga, and Sexburga have their shrines outside our counties ; but Withburga has hers—where the poet Cowper has his—at East Dereham. In the early pages of *Lavengro* George Borrow speaks of them both. His words about Cowper end thus : " No longer at early dawn does the sexton of the old church reverently doff his hat as, supported by some kind friend, the death-stricken creature totters along the church path to that mouldering edifice with the low roof enclosing a spring of sanatory waters, built and devoted to some saint—if the legend over the door be true—by the daughter of an East Anglian king." (The saint and the king's daughter are, of course, really one and the same person.)

St. Withburg's Well is indeed in the churchyard, where the ground slopes away at the west end of the church, and the waters

still have some repute for healing. The only picturesque thing that
is told of St. Withburg is that a white doe used to furnish her with
milk, and with a doe she is represented on perhaps four Norfolk rood-
screens. The modern inscription over the well records the translation
of her body to Ely, to keep company with Etheldreda and Sexburga.
It was the fate of many local saints to gravitate towards the great
abbeys : stories of relic-stealing are familiar, and I fear this was a
bad case. Abbot Brithnoth, of Ely, about the year 974, visited
Dereham with an armed train, made a great feast for the men of
Dereham, and when they were in post-prandial sleep stole the body
and fled. Reaching Brandon unmolested, they took boat, only just
in time. The Dereham men and their neighbours were in pursuit
and lined the river banks ; there was wild tumult, and darts were
thrown. Only by urging on the boatmen to top speed could the
abbot make good his escape.

On the very edge of Suffolk is the village of Exning, parent of the
New Market which has sprung up on the high-road a little way off.
At Exning the site of a palace of Saxon kings is pointed out, and
near it, on ground now the property of the Jockey Club, is something
that is marked on the maps as St. Mindred's Well. It is more than
a well : it is a set of three groups of springs welling up visibly in pools
which are inlets in a steep wooded bank—a very pretty and uncommon place, quite secluded and quiet. Local people say that
St. Etheldreda was baptized there, which seems unlikely, and that
the water is good for ailments of the eyes, which may be true. But
who St. Mindred was nobody can tell. The best guess is that she
is identical with St. Wendreda, patroness of the church at March.
But this takes us very little farther, for nobody knows a single fact
about St. Wendreda. Still, there is St. Mindred's Well, a saint's well,
and worth a word, for it is known but to very few.

All the persons I have hitherto mentioned belong to the seventh
century and to the first generations of East Anglian Christians. I
believe that the eighth century has but one saint to offer us, and his
cult has become attached rather to the west than the east of England.
I mean St. Ethelbert, a young king of the East Angles, whom the
great Offa of Mercia caused to be beheaded at his palace of Sutton
Walls, near Hereford. The deed is a principal blot upon Offa's
record. The reasons for it are obscure. Offa's queen is credited

with having persuaded her husband that Ethelbert, who had come ostensibly to court the king's daughter, was really spying out the land. It was thought that Offa's remorse for this murder was one cause of his journeying to Rome, and that it also influenced him to undertake such works of piety as the founding of St. Albans Abbey. Ethelbert became the patron of Hereford, but a good many churches are dedicated to him in Norfolk and Suffolk, and he appears on at least one rood-screen, at Burnham Norton.

The ninth century gives us the most famous of all East Anglian saints, in the person of St. Edmund, King and Martyr, who died at the hands of the Danes in the year 870.

We are indebted to Lord Francis Hervey for having (in his book

NORTON, SUFFOLK, MISERICORDE—"THE MARTYRDOM OF ST. EDMUND"

Corolla S. Eadmundi and elsewhere) disengaged the story of this gallant young prince and true martyr from many late misrepresentations. The most widely current form of his legend tells us that he was born in Germany, and was the younger son of a king, Alkmund of Saxony. Offa, king of East Anglia, visited his father's house when on pilgrimage to Jerusalem, and was much taken with the boy. Falling ill on his return journey from Jerusalem, and feeling that death was near, he charged his nobles to receive Edmund as his successor in the kingdom. So Edmund takes leave of his parents, lands at Hunstanton, is crowned at Bures, and rules wisely and well till the crisis of the Danish invasion. The beginning of this story, says Lord Francis, will not do. There is no discoverable Offa of East Anglia, and the foreign birth of Edmund is not only improbable in itself but contradicted by other quite old forms of the legend. In Lord Francis's own view Edmund was nephew to Athelstan, king of Kent, and was the son of a prominent Kentish alderman, Ealhhere ; but whether that is so or not, Edmund was English-born—born about 841 and succeeding in 855.

Next we have an episode of the wrecking of Ragnar Lodbrog on Edmund's land, of Beorn the treacherous huntsman murdering him, and as a punishment being sent out to sea in a boat, cast up on the shores of Denmark, and persuading the sons of Lodbrog, Ingwar and Ubba, to avenge their father's death on Edmund. This is folk-lore : the elements of the tale are found in other surroundings. But true it is that Ingwar, Ubba, Beorn and Guthrum did land in East Anglia in 866. At first they did not ravage that land much ; they went northward and plundered there and in Mercia : it was not until 870 that they collided with Edmund. The phases of the struggle are not clear, but the record of its conclusion, as far as Edmund is concerned, rests on good authority. The armour-bearer of St. Edmund was an eye-witness of his end ; of his refusal to bargain with the Danes and renounce his faith ; of his being evil entreated, scourged, and shot with arrows, and finally beheaded, at a place called Hægelisdun. This man lived to be very old, and to tell the story of what he had seen in the hearing of the great king Æthelstan. Dunstan, then quite young, heard it, and remembered it well, being moved to tears at the recital ; and three years before his own death repeated it to the learned foreign monk, Abbo of Fleury, who embodied it in his *Passion of St. Edmund*, and in a dedicatory letter to Dunstan records the circumstances I have told. Dunstan was born, not in 925, as used to be believed, but more probably in 909 : the old soldier very likely told the story to the king in 929 (when Æthelstan visited several of the shrines of England), so Dunstan would have been about twenty, and a very competent witness.

Now as to the place of the great conflict and martyrdom. The following statements, which will be found in the *Dictionary of National Biography*, represent the current belief. Edmund was martyred at a village near Heglisdune (Hill of Eagles), afterwards called Hoxne. His body was buried at Hoxne in a wooden chapel, and rested there for thirty-three years. The tree at which tradition declared him to have been slain stood in the park at Hoxne until 1849, when it fell.

HADLEIGH ; THE DEANERY TOWERS.

In the course of breaking it up an arrow-head was found embedded in the trunk.

Lord Francis Hervey points out that Heglisdune or Hægelisdun does not mean Hill of Eagles (eagle is a French word), and cannot be twisted into connexion with Hoxne ; that a Bury writer earlier than 1100 tells us that Edmund was buried, not at Hoxne, but at a village called Suthtune, near the place of his martyrdom ; and that when " St. Edmund's Oak " fell (in 1848) a Suffolk resident, writing to the *Gentleman's Magazine*, denied, on the strength of fifty years' knowledge of the district, that any oak at Hoxne was traditionally connected with the martyrdom or known as St. Edmund's Oak.

It cannot be denied that old tradition did associate the martyrdom with Hoxne, and that there was a chapel of St. Edmund there in the eleventh century (as there was also, curiously enough, a church of St. Ethelbert). But the statement of the Bury writer is older than any written record of the Hoxne tradition, and is derived, he tells us, from the " telling of our ancestors." We have seen that he mentions Suthtune or Sutton as the first burial-place of his patron. The only Sutton in Suffolk is one near Woodbridge, and it is in that district, and more especially in the locality called Staverton Forest which adjoins Sutton, that Lord Francis would place the conflict with the Danes, and the martyrdom.

I will not follow in detail the removals of St. Edmund's body first to Beaduricesworth (Bury), then, under pressure of invasion, to London, and back to Bury, on which last transit it quite probably left a trace of its passage in the wooden church of Greenstead in Essex. But a word on a comparatively recent episode may be allowed. In 1901 certain relics were obtained from the Canons of St. Sernin's Church at Toulouse to be reposited in the Westminster Cathedral, then newly built. They were said to be the relics of St. Edmund. Since the seventeenth century Toulouse ecclesiastics had from time to time ventilated a story that in 1216 the Dauphin Louis, on his raid into England, had carried off the body of St. Edmund from his abbey and presented it to the church of St. Sernin. Few people who had given any attention to this legend had failed to see how very shadowy it was, how totally destitute of contemporary authority, and how impossible to reconcile with known facts. When the matter was discussed in *The Times*, the Roman Catholic authorities in this

2

country reconsidered the position, and eventually the relics were returned to Toulouse (if they do not still repose at Arundel). The true relics may, I believe, be just possibly discoverable beneath the floor of the crypt of the Abbey church, which has never been properly explored.

One or two rather shadowy saint figures are associated with St. Edmund : the bishop Humbert who perished on the same day as the king ; Edwold, reputed brother of Edmund, who retired to lead a hermit's life at or near Cerne, in Dorset, and was honoured at Cerne—of these we have no trace ; Fremund, cousin to Edmund, who avenged his death by killing 40,000 Danes at Retford, and was assassinated in the moment of victory. Lydgate tells his story in his metrical *Life of St. Edmund :* he was the great saint of Dunstable Priory ; but his very existence is highly problematic.

The cult of St. Edmund was widespread ; there are well over fifty churches dedicated to him in this country ; he has chapels in the churches of Westminster, Tewkesbury, and Wells. The Crusaders built him a church at Damietta in 1220 ; you will find a window of his life in the north transept of Amiens Cathedral. In England there are perhaps a dozen wall-paintings of his martyrdom, and his effigy is on some twenty rood-screens. Two splendid copies of Lydgate's metrical *Life* exist, the finer in the British Museum (Harley MS. 2278), the other in private hands. Older and more splendid is a twelfth-century MS. of his life with many pictures, written at Bury, which belonged to Sir George Holford and last year crossed the Atlantic to Mr. Pierpont Morgan's library.

The most famous episode connected with him, apart from his martyrdom, was his appearance after death to the Danish king Sweyn, whom he rebuked for ravaging his lands and smote with his spear, so that on the morrow he died. There were many representations of this in the Abbey church.

Only a few more saints remain to be noticed, and they are rather abnormal. The first is St. William of Norwich, a boy who was said to have been murdered—scourged, crowned with thorns, and more or less crucified by the Jews of Norwich on March 24, 1144. Nearly forty years ago I found, in an old parochial library at Brent Eleigh, the unique MS. of his life and miracles written by Thomas of Monmouth, a Norwich monk, in the twelfth century, and edited it in collaboration with Dr. Jessopp (1896). The find was of appreciable importance, for William is the first of a lamentably long series of boys said to have been martyred by Jews in derision of our Lord ; the slander still crops up now and again in Eastern Europe, and in its time has wrought terrible mischief in the way of massacres and injustices. St. William's body found a home in Norwich Cathedral ; his chapel still exists under the organ loft. Perhaps half a dozen rood-screens in Norfolk and Suffolk show his picture.

Then in 1181 Bury made its effort to rival St. William. A boy named Robert met his end at the hands of the Jews ; Jocelin de Brakelond, the Bury chronicler, tells us of him, and says that he wrote his story. We have it not, and only one clue to his legend remains, in a MS. in the collection of Mr. Dyson Perrins, of Malvern. In this is a fifteenth-century picture in four compartments, showing (1) an old woman putting the boy's body into a well ; (2) the body lying near a tree, angels taking up his soul, a man shooting an arrow into the tree ; (3) a cleric kneeling in prayer with a scroll addressing St. Robert ; (4) a robin, painted on something that looks like a charter or deed. The robin must be an allusion to Robert's name : without the text of the legend we cannot properly interpret the rest, but it is evident that an old woman was concerned, and that she tried in vain to conceal the boy's body. Among the minor poems of Lydgate the Bury monk is an invocation to St. Robert.

Third is St. Walstan of Bawburgh, not far from Norwich. His parents were a (mythical) king and queen residing at Blythburgh ; his mother Blida also attained saintship and had a chapel at Martham. Walstan renounced the world and left his parents to take service with a farmer at Taverham. The farmer's wife was rather harsh to him, but his industry and excellence won over both husband and wife, and they offered to make him their heir ; this he refused, but asked for " the burden of a cow " that was in calf. Two calves were born, and thrived amazingly in Walstan's care. Time passed on, and one day as he ploughed he heard angels singing and prophesying to him the day of his death. He called his fellow labourer, but *he* could hear nothing till he set his foot upon Walstan's, and then the heavens were opened to his vision and he heard the bells ringing. That same Saturday the farmer heard the missing prince cried at Norwich market, guessed that Walstan was he, and hurried home, only to be told by Walstan that he would die on the Monday, and this he did, receiving the last rites in the field, and praying for all sick persons and cattle. His own oxen drew his body to Bawburgh Church ; they crossed the Wensum as on dry land—the wheel tracks are still seen on the surface of the water. Three springs of water rose at places where they halted : the church wall opened to receive the cortège. Down to the Reformation labourers came to Bawburgh once a year to obtain blessings for themselves and their beasts ; which makes Bishop Bale unkindly compare Walstan to Pan and Priapus.

The chapel or aisle at Bawburgh which contained the shrine is gone : it may have joined the north-west wall of the church, which is a very humble building. One of the miraculous springs is still in being, in a farm below the church. There seem to be about six pictures of St. Walstan, all of them on Norfolk rood-screens. He is represented with his two oxen at his feet, and usually has a scythe. His mother, St. Blida, occurs twice. Walstan seems a mythical personage. I have wondered if St. Blida is not equally unsubstantial, and a mistake for St. Bride, who also appears on a few screens.

Our two counties contain in the imagery of their churches (especially the screen paintings) a good many indications of the evolution of popular devotion at the end of the mediæval period, and perhaps more particularly of the foreign, mainly Flemish, influence that was at work in those parts. To this last I should assign the appearance of such persons as SS. Barbara, Dorothy, Clare, Elizabeth of Thuringia, Erasmus, Gertrude, Jeron, Gudula, perhaps the three Maries, certainly the plague-saints Rochus and Sebastian ; also Sitha, Theobald, and Wilgefort ; and the very odd occurrence of a small picture of the Temptation of St. Anthony on the screen at Tacolnestone.

Some indigenous figures also, not yet mentioned, crop up : notably King Henry VI (about nine times), St. John of Bridlington (once), and that mysterious being Sir John Shorne (four times). He was Rector of North Marston in Bucks at the end of the thirteenth century, had a chapel in St. George's, Windsor, and was invoked against ague ; but his only known act was to conjure the devil into a boot, the occasion and sequelæ of this being alike unknown. It is with the accompaniments of devil and boot that we see him on the rood-screens. He is puzzling enough, but still more puzzling is a personage

BROMHOLM PRIORY; BACTON.

LITCHAM; CHURCH CHEST.

whom we meet but once, on the screen at Gateley, Sancta Puella Ridibowne ; she bears no attribute—her name inscribed below her, though perhaps retouched, is quite plain. She may have been a maiden of strictly local celebrity (like another I have heard of, St. Margaret of Hoveton), or just possibly she may have been one Christina of Redburne, near St. Albans, of whom there is a Life.

We can now pass to Relics, in writing of which I have in mind those imported relics which attracted pilgrims to the places in which they were kept. The importing of relics began in very early times. Already in the seventh century Benedict Biscop, on one or more of his many journeys to Rome, brought back to Wearmouth " relics of Christ's blessed Apostles and Martyrs," but these hardly became objects of pilgrimage ; nor did those, highly valued though they were, which king Æthelstan, a great collector, accumulated in the tenth century. A church would greatly plume itself on the possession of them, but things like the Water-pots of Cana or the stones of Stephen's martyrdom were rather museum pieces than efficacious to do cures : greatly inferior to the bones of a patronal saint. It was even, I think, mainly to dignify the church and attract worshippers that an Abbot of Evesham purchased the body of St. Odulf and an Abbot of Peterborough that of St. Florentinus at great prices. But when the crusading period sets in, the case is altered. Great curative efficacy is attributed to those relics—particularly those connected with the Passion— which were brought from Constantinople after the shameful plundering by the Latins in 1204. One such relic at least made its way to Norfolk—the Rood of Bromholm or Bacton. Bromholm was a small and poor Cluniac house founded in 1113 : to it some time before the year 1223 came a cleric who had been chaplain to Baldwin of Constantinople. On the report of his master's death in 1206 he fled to England with all the relics he could lay hands on, and two sons. He went hawking these relics about to several monasteries, asking that his sons should be provided for in the establishment. Among the treasures was a wooden cross almost as wide as a man's hand, a portion of the True Cross. The St. Albans monks would not have it, though they did buy some jewellery and two of St. Margaret's fingers. Nor were the other houses he approached satisfied with his account of the Cross. But they of Bromholm took it readily, and were richly repaid for their trustfulness : no less than thirty-nine dead people were raised to life ; blind, lame, lepers, demoniacs, were healed ; pilgrims came from all parts of England and from overseas, and from obscurity and poverty the monastery became rich, and equipped itself with buildings of which the remains show the fine quality. We have some notion of the appearance of the relic, for in the fifteenth century it was customary to sell to visitors small pictures of the Rood, a double cross with a little crucifix-figure : one or two of these have survived, inserted into books of devotion. When we read in Foxe's *Martyrs* of a man being prosecuted for burning the Rood of Bromholm, we may be sure that what he burnt was one of these pictures, not the Rood itself, for nothing is made of the case.

The other great pilgrimage-place of Norfolk was Walsingham. It was an Augustinian house founded some time in the twelfth century in connexion with a Chapel of the Virgin, which had been built (in 1061) by a lady Richoldis, or Richeldis, mother of the founder, Geoffrey de Favraches. This chapel came to be the great attraction of the place. It was apparently a small wooden structure over which later a protective stone casing was built, and somehow the belief grew up that it had been built by angels under the direction of the Virgin herself, and was a copy of the *Santa Casa* at Nazareth. Then it was said that, now that the Holy Land was in possession of the Saracens, the Virgin had forsaken her holy house at Nazareth for the English sanctuary ; finally, that it actually was the *Santa Casa*, transported to England by angels, the Loreto legend being simply borrowed. How the claims of the two sanctuaries were adjusted I do not know. But there is no doubt about the celebrity of that of Walsingham. As late as 1534 the offerings made in the chapel amounted to £201 in the year, whereas the contributions to the other great relic of the place, the milk of the Virgin, only totalled £2 2s. 3d. Famous as Walsingham was in the old days, it derives its chief notoriety now from one who hardly meant to advertise it, Erasmus, whose account of his visits to Walsingham and Canterbury, in the dialogue *Peregrinatio Religionis ergo,* is a classic too hackneyed for quotation.

I do not find that other notable relics attracted pilgrims to Norfolk and Suffolk. Thetford and Ipswich both owned rather famous images of the Virgin ; Lynn has its remarkable Red Mount Chapel, built to contain a relic of the Virgin ; but to such places as Castle Acre, Binham, Wymondham, St. Benet's Hulme, Butley, or Leiston, there does not seem to have been any concourse of strangers : the religious life went on there in a tranquil and I dare say humdrum fashion.

So the incorrupt body of St. Edmund, the Walsingham Chapel, and the Rood of Bromholm stand out as the three special objects of veneration in East Anglia.

MONASTERIES

ONE very important feature in the survey of any region of England is the number and character of its monastic foundations. I have thought it worth while therefore to draw up a list—a little *Monasticon* of Norfolk and Suffolk—which comprises all the foundations which can properly be called monastic. I have omitted those early monasteries which perished in the Danish invasion, and were never refounded ; and I have taken no account of hospitals or hermitages.

A few general observations may serve to give some actuality to the bare list of names. First, as to the various Orders represented. The premier Order is that of St. Benedict (denoted by the letters O.S.B.), founded in the sixth century, and introduced into England, as we believe, by St. Augustine, though centuries elapsed between his coming and the final regularizing of the monastic life according to the Rule of the Founder. That work was done in the tenth century, and the great movers in it were St. Dunstan and St. Æthelwold of Winchester, with whom may be joined St. Oswald of York and Worcester.

The oldest Benedictine house in these counties which subsisted through the Middle Ages is that of St. Benet's Hulme, which was rebuilt (in 955) after its destruction by the Danes, and from which Cnut transferred monks to colonize Bury Abbey, which was the most famous house in the two counties. The Benedictines were commonly known as the Black Monks.

The later monastic Orders (I am not speaking of Friars) were usually the offspring of successive efforts to reform and tighten up the observance of the Benedictine rule. The first of these was the Cluniac, originating about 912. All the houses of this Order were directly dependent on the mother house of Cluny (near Mâcon), though in this country the bonds were gradually relaxed. There were thirty-two Cluniac houses in England at the Dissolution : five in Norfolk, of which Bromholm, Castleacre, and Thetford were important ; two inconsiderable ones in Suffolk.

The Cistercians, dating we may say from 1092, were far more numerous in England than the Cluniacs : their houses numbered 100. But in Norfolk and Suffolk they are hardly represented : this region was a populous one, and the Order preferred to settle in wild and uncultivated districts ; hence the large number of great Cistercian houses in Yorkshire, Wales, and Scotland, whereas Norfolk can show but one nunnery and Suffolk one abbey. This Order was known as that of the White or Grey Monks.

Of another famous Order, the Carthusians, all England had but eight houses, and our counties none. From monks we pass to Canons Regular, of which we reckon three Orders ; but the transition is slight, and the distinction becomes negligible. The Rule which governed the most important of them was attributed to St. Augustine of Hippo, but the letter or tract of his which contains its principles needed a great deal of codifying and comment to reduce it into a Rule. The Augustinian Order, which did not come to England before 1108, numbered eventually some 170 houses of canons and nuns, of which twenty-nine were in our counties, Walsingham being by far the most famous. The Austin Canons were known as Black Canons. A branch of this Order, the Canons of the Holy Sepulchre, I mention because among the few houses they had in England one was at Thetford. They wore the Augustinian habit, with a double cross on the cloak.

The Premonstratensian is the second of our Orders ; its imposing name comes from the locality called Prémontré, near Laon ; the date of foundation is 1119, the founder is St. Norbert. These White Canons, as they were called, had thirty-four houses in England, and of these Leiston, the only one in Suffolk, was perhaps the most considerable in our district. Norfolk had three.

The third of the Canons' Orders is the Gilbertine, the only Order ever founded in England ; outside England it never spread. The founder was St. Gilbert of Sempringham (Yorks) ; the houses contained both men and women. Of thirteen establishments, one, Shouldham, was in Norfolk.

The Military Orders—Templars and Hospitallers—are negligible. The Templars are said to have had preceptories at Battisford, Dunwich, and Gislingham, which passed, like the rest of their property, to the Hospitallers.

The Friars close the list.   Monks and friars are very different persons, as I hope most people nowadays realize, though but a few generations ago it was not so.   In spite of Friar Tuck, whom Scott places in Richard I's time, there were no friars in England before 1221, when the Black Friars or Dominicans came.   The Grey Friars (Franciscans) followed in 1224.   These, the two great Orders of Friars, were founded by famous and historic persons.   The next most important was that of the Carmelites, or White Friars, who chose to shroud their origins in mystery, and traced themselves back to the Prophet Elijah.   They came to England about 1240.

The Austin Friars were made out of several lesser Orders, amalgamated in 1265 by Clement IV.   Two such lesser Orders were represented in England, viz. the Friars of the Sack and the Pied Friars. The sole house of the latter in England was at Norwich, and so was the single house of the Friars of the Sack in these counties.   The Crouched, Crutched, or Crossed Friars had also one little house, at Great Whelnetham.

Of the greater Orders the houses were almost always to be found in towns.   Thus in Norfolk there were Black and Grey and White Friars at Lynn, Norwich, and Yarmouth ; Black Friars at Thetford ; Grey at Walsingham ; Austin Friars at Lynn, Norwich, Thetford, and Walsingham ; and White Friars at two smaller places, Blakeney and Burnham Norton.   In Suffolk, Ipswich had Black, Grey, and White ; Dunwich, Black and Grey ; Bury, Grey ; Clare and Gorleston had Austin Friars.

The Minoresses or Franciscan nuns had but three houses in the whole country : one of these, Bruisyard, was in Suffolk.

A further explanation of two terms which occur in the list is perhaps needed.   Several houses are described as a " cell to " another place : this means, of course, that they were dependencies of the said place, some quite large, as Binham, and still more Wymondham, which latter belonged to St. Albans for the greater part of its life.   Such places were governed by a prior appointed by the mother house. Others were small establishments with only a few monks, some of whom might have been banished from the mother house for misconduct.

DUNWICH, SUFFOLK.   THE FRIARY GATEWAYS

Then there is frequent mention of alien priories. These also were cells, but cells to houses in France. At and after the Conquest the Norman nobles often conferred on their home-abbeys some part of the lands they had won in England. Bec, famous for its connexion with Lanfranc and Anselm, was perhaps the greatest owner of English land. More than once in the French wars the English kings confiscated these alien priories. Some few of the largest were " made denizen," that is, cut off from their allegiance to a French house and gifted with independence. Then, in the course of our wars with France, all the alien priories fell to the Crown. Henry VI, being a really pious man, would not put these new possessions to selfish or secular uses, but employed many of them in the endowment of his two great colleges of Eton and King's ; hence the frequent entry of " granted to Eton " or " to King's."

Of many of the houses in my list the remains now visible are very scanty ; and, from the picturesque point of view, it is unfortunate that the buildings, being in a country where good stone was not indigenous, have served as quarries, have been stripped of their stone facings, and reduced to masses of flint rubble in many cases. Very few churches have survived in any degree of completeness. We have the Cathedral of Norwich, and we have the naves of Binham and Wymondham. Also we have a rarity in the shape of the Black Friar's Church at Norwich, of which the nave is well known as St. Andrew's Hall, and the choir long served as the Dutch church. Of the ruined monasteries that of Bury takes precedence in both counties, and in Norfolk Castleacre is considerably the most attractive ; Thetford is full of ruins, and Butley, Leiston, Walsingham, and Bromholm, all have something more than common to show.

There are not many of the sites which lend themselves to the study of monastic life in detail, but those of Norwich, Bury, and Castleacre at least are instructive, in so far as they allow the disposition of the main buildings—church, cloister, chapter-house, refectory, dormitory, infirmary—to be traced by even the inexperienced eye. Without going into minute detail let it be said that the buildings I have mentioned were the essential ones in any monastery, and were arranged on a uniform plan. South of the church (where possible), and attached to its nave, was the four-sided cloister ; out of this, on the east side, opened the chapter-house, the daily meeting-place of the monks ; over the eastern walk was the dormitory (dorter), from which there was access to the church for the night services. Along the side opposite to the church (the south side, normally) ran the refectory (frater). A passage from the east side led to the infirmary (farmery), which was a building in the form of a church, the eastern portion being its chapel. The west side of the cloister usually had store-houses or the like along it or over it.

One further word of caution, which I have found necessary. It is a common habit to use the word convent as if it meant a nunnery. There is no reason in this. The word means the body of members of the house, the people as distinguished from the buildings.

SUFFOLK

Place.	Order.	Remarks.
Alnesbourne (nr. Ipswich) .	Aug.	
Babwell, *see* Bury.		
Blakenham . . .	O.S.B.	Alien priory, cell to Bec. Granted to Eton Coll.
Blythburgh . . .	Aug.	
Bricett	O.S.B.	Alien priory, cell to Nobiliac (nr. Limoges). Granted to King's Coll., Camb.
Bruisyard. . . .	Franciscan nuns	
Bungay	O.S.B. nuns	
Bury St. Edmund . .	O.S.B. Abbey	
Babwell	Franciscans	
Butley	Aug.	
Campsey Ashe . . .	Aug. nuns	
Chipley (in Poslingford) .	Aug.	Annexed to Stoke College.
Clare	Aug. Friars	
Coddenham . . .	O.S.B. nuns	Cell.
Creeting St. Mary . .	O.S.B.	Alien priory, cell to Grestein.
Creeting St. Olave . .	O.S.B.	Alien priory, cell to Bernay. Both granted to Eton.
Dodnash (in Bentley parish) .	Aug.	
Dunwich	O.S.B.	Cell to Eye.
,, ...	Dominicans (Black Friars)	
,, ...	Franciscans (Grey Friars)	

BURY ST. EDMUNDS; THE 12TH CENTURY TOWER.

Place.	Order.	Remarks.
Eye	O.S.B.	Once a cell to Bernay.
Felixstowe	O.S.B.	Cell to Rochester.
Flixton	Aug. nuns	
Gislingham . . .	Templars (and Hospitallers)	
Gorleston	Austin Friars	
Herringfleet . . .	Aug.	
Ipswich, Holy Trinity . .	Aug.	
,, St. Peter's . .	Aug.	Dissolved by Wolsey for his College.
,, ...	Dominicans	
,, ...	Franciscans	
,, ...	Carmelites	
Ixworth	Aug.	
Kersey . . .	O.S.B.	Granted to King's Coll., Camb.
Leiston	Premonstr.	
Letheringham . . .	Aug.	
Mendham	Cluniac	
Orford	Aug.	
Redlingfield . . .	O.S.B. nuns	
Rumburgh ' . . .	O.S.B.	Cell to St. Benet's Hulme; then to St. Mary's, York.
Sibton	Cisterc.	
Snape	Aug.	Cell to Colchester.
Stoke-by-Clare . . .	O.S.B.	Alien priory, cell to Bec.
Sudbury, St. Bartholomew .	O.S.B.	Cell to Westminster.
,, ...	Dominicans	
Thetford, *see* Norfolk.		
Wangford, nr. Reydon . .	Cluniac	Cell to Thetford.
Whelnetham (Great) . .	Crouched Friars	
Woodbridge . . .	Aug.	

NORFOLK

Aldeby	O.S.B.	Cell to Norwich.
Beeston	O.S.B.	Alien priory, cell to St. Begare in Brittany.
St. Benet's Hulme . .	O.S.B. Abbey	
Binham	O.S.B.	Cell to St. Albans.
Blackborough (nr. Middleton)	O.S.B. nuns	
Blakeney	Carmelite (White Friars)	
Bromehill (at Weeting) .	Aug. (Black Canons)	

Place.		Order.	Remarks.
Bromholm (or Bacton)	.	Cluniac	
Buckenham . . .		Aug.	
Burnham Norton .	.	Carmelite	
Carrow (by Norwich) .	.	O.S.B. nuns	
Castleacre		Cluniac	
Cokesford (in East Rudham)		Aug.	
Crabhouse (at Wiggenhall, St. Mary Magdalene)		Aug. nuns	
Creake, North . .	.	Aug.	
Custhorpe . . .	.	Aug.	Cell to Westacre.
Dereham, West . .	.	Premonstr. (White Canons)	
Docking . . .	.	O.S.B.	Alien priory, cell to Ivry. Granted to Eton.
Field Dalling . .	.		Alien priory, cell to Savigny.
Flitcham . . .	.	Aug.	
Heacham . . .	.	Cluniac	Cell to Lewes.
Hempton (by Fakenham)	.	Aug.	
Haveringland, or Mountjoy	.	Aug.	Cell to Wymondham.
Hickling . . .	.	Aug.	
Horsham St. Faith	.	O.S.B.	
Horstead . .	.	O.S.B.	Cell to Caen (nuns).
Langley . . .	.	Premonstr.	
Lessingham . .	.	O.S.B.	Alien priory, cell to Bec. Granted to King's Coll., Camb.
Lynn, King's . .	.	Dominicans	
,, ,, . .	.	Franciscans	
,, ,, . .	.	Carmelites	
,, ,, . .	.	Austin Friars	
Marham . . .	.	Cisterc. nuns	
Massingham, Great .	.	Aug.	
Modney (nr. Hilgay) .	.	O.S.B.	Cell to Ramsey.
Monks Toft, *see* Toft Monks	.		
Norwich, Cathedral Priory	.	O.S.B.	
,, . . .	.	Dominicans	
,, . . .	.	Franciscans	
,, . . .	.	Carmelites	
,, . . .	.	Austin Friars	
,, . . .	.	Friars of the Sack	
,, . . .	.	Pied Friars	
Pentney . . .	.	Aug.	
Sheringham . .	.	Aug.	Cell to Nutley (Bucks).

Place.				Order.	Remarks.
Shouldham	.	.	.	Gilbertine	
Slevesholm	.	.	.	Cluniac	Cell to Castleacre.
Sporle	.	.	.	O.S.B.	Alien priory, cell to St. Florent, Saumur. Granted to Eton.
Stow	.	.	.	Cluniac	Cell to Castleacre.
Thetford	.	.	.	Cluniac	
,,	.	.	.	O.S.B. nuns	
,,	.	.	.	Austin Canons of the Holy Sepulchre	
,,	.	.	.	Dominicans	
,,	.	.	.	Austin Friars	
Toft Monks	.	.	.	O.S.B.	Alien priory, cell to Préaux. Granted to King's Coll., Camb.
Weybourn	.	.	.	Aug.	
Walsingham	.	.	.	Aug.	
,,		.	.	Austin Friars	
,,		.	.	Franciscans	
Wendling	.	.	.	Premonstr.	
Wereham St. Winwaloe			.	O.S.B., then Premonstr.	Formerly alien priory, then cell to West Dereham.
Westacre	.	.	.	Aug.	
Weybridge (in Acle)	.	.	.	Aug.	
Wormegay	.	.	.	Aug.	Cell to Pentney.
Wymondham	.	.	.	O.S.B.	Cell to St. Albans till 1447.
Witchingham	.	.	.	O.S.B.	Alien priory, cell to Longueville.
Yarmouth	.	.	.	Dominicans	
,,	.	.	.	Franciscans	
,,	.	.	.	Carmelites	

SUFFOLK

BURY ST. EDMUNDS AND ENVIRONS

WE will enter Suffolk from Cambridge by the Newmarket line. Within reach of Newmarket (of which I have nothing to say) is *Exning*, with St. Mindred's Well, described above (p. 14), and also another remarkable little place which until recently was in Suffolk, but now I believe belongs to Cambridgeshire, *Landwade*, long the seat of the Cottons—off the road, and consisting merely of church, ancient farmhouse, and moated site of a large mansion. The church, a cruciform building of 1445, is unrestored and little used, and contains good woodwork—roof, seats, screen—and considerable fragments of fifteenth-century glass : a St. Margaret is very notable ; there are also remains of a series of Apostles.

Reverting to the Newmarket–Cambridge line we observe that on the left—northwards—we soon get into the open heathy country, of which Mildenhall is the centre, and which borders on the fen ; and on the right—southwards—find a more hilly and wooded region containing the highest ground in Suffolk : 420 ft., in the parish of *Rede*, is the county's best achievement. Of places near the line, *Kennett* on the north has recently discovered wall-paintings : one of the Three Dead and Three Living, a *memento mori* subject which may well have become popular in the years after the Black Death, though it was invented earlier. The scene is of three kings or young knights who are out hawking and pass a churchyard, where they meet three terrible corpses, hideous with the ravages of death, who say to them, " As we are, so will you be."

Great Saxham, on the south, has some remarkable foreign glass in its east and west windows ; the latter, in the tower, is filled with small late subjects, mostly Swiss, and of the seventeenth century. In the east window the glass is earlier (16th cent.) and of finer quality. It has a marriage scene (probably of Tobias and Sara), part of a Circumcision, an *Ecce Homo*, and the Virgin and the Son interceding for mankind with the Father, a heathenish subject which was adopted

in the book called the *Mirror of
Man's Salvation*, but was invented by a twelfth-century
divine, Arnold of Bonneval.
Notice also the bust of John
Eldred (1632), whose travels
are in Hakluyt, and whose
epitaph is worth reading.

Little Saxham has the best of
the round towers in Suffolk.
The Norman arcading round
the top storey is very rich.
When you enter, note the Norman recess beside the tower
arch. A chapel north of the
chancel has stately monuments,
those of Sir Thomas Lucas
(*temp.* Henry VII) and William
the only Baron Crofts (1677).
The popeys of the seats have
the dogs, ducks, pelicans,
dragons, which will be met
again and again.

Risby, just north of the line,
has another good round tower,
and bits of old glass, enough
to show that there was a series
of Apostles and Prophets, and a
screen, and some wall-paintings.

Ickworth lies on the south,
in a great park. Ickworth
Building, a landmark to the
neighbourhood, is an immense
low-domed structure begun by
that Earl of Bristol who was
Bishop of Derry (*d.* 1803), and
was meant to contain collections
which he made in Italy and

ICKWORTH CHURCH, SUFFOLK:
FRESCO IN CHANCEL

3

which never got to England. The church has several interesting objects : a very fine double piscina (13th cent.); a collection of panels of foreign glass in several windows (16th and 17th cents.). Some of the subjects are very unusual. In a window north of nave we have the Priests of Bel feasting ; the Jews sending Mary Magdalene, Martha, Lazarus, and others out to sea in a boat ; Daniel showing the king the footsteps of Bel's priests. In another south of chancel are the Trojan horse, the Temptation of St. Anthony, and one or two subjects which baffled me. Perhaps most remarkable is a wall-painting (13th cent.) of an angel on the east wall, south of altar : part of Annunciation.

So we come to *Bury St. Edmunds*, which may be used as a centre for a good part of the west of the county.

It is not part of my plan to write a systematic guide to the larger towns, but to concentrate on special features. At Bury the great feature is the Abbey and its precinct. The site of the Abbey is now laid out in gardens, some public, some private. A short piece of historical introduction, and then we will examine the remains. St. Edmund, we have seen, was martyred in 870, and his body remained near the place of the martyrdom for upwards of thirty years. Then it was removed to Bury, at that time known as Beauricesworth (after an unknown settler Beauric), and there was guarded by a small body of clerics in a wooden church of large dimensions : to these clerics King Edmund, son of Edward the Elder, gave lands in 945. In 1010 Danish pirates landed at Ipswich, and in alarm the guardian Egelwin removed the body to London, where it remained about three years, and was carried back to what we may now call Bury. In 1014 the Danish king Sweyn died ; it was believed at the hands of St. Edmund. His son Cnut in 1028 gave a generous charter of liberties to the guardians of the shrine, who, be it noted, were now no longer secular clergy, but monks of the Benedictine Order. The seculars were turned out in 1020 by Ælfwin, Bishop of Elmham, and replaced by twenty monks from St. Benet's Hulme and from Ely. Uvius, prior of Hulme, became the first Abbot of Bury. A stone church was built by Cnut and consecrated in 1032. To Edward the Confessor (*d.* 1066) the Abbey owed the grant of jurisdiction over eight and a half hundreds in the county, as well as the great manor of Mildenhall. The Abbey life was now fairly started. The great

YAXLEY; DETAIL OF PORCH.

ORFORD CHURCH.

rulers of the place in its first two centuries were Baldwin of St. Denis
(1065–97), Anselm, nephew of the saint (1119–48), Samson, made
famous by Carlyle (1182–1213). The crises of its story were the
peasants' risings of 1327 and 1381, a great fire in 1465 which gutted
the interior of the church, and the Dissolution in 1538.

Now as to the history of the buildings. The church of which we
see the remains was a great Norman building at least 500 ft. long.
The eastern part was built by Abbot Baldwin (d. 1097) ; there was
a crypt under it, and at the east end three apsidal (round-ended)
chapels projected from the main apse. After 1102 the sacrist
Godefrid, a man of large body and large ideas, continued the work
westward, widening the building a little, and setting up the four
great piers of the central tower, of which there are remains. He
must also have built a good deal of the transepts, which had an aisle
on the eastern side. After 1119 two sacrists, Ralph and Hervé,
built the nave, of twelve bays. After 1182 Samson completed the
west end. The largest addition made in later times was the Lady
Chapel, north of the choir, begun by Simon de Luton in 1275.

When it was finished, the church resembled in some respects Ely
Cathedral ; for like Ely it had at the west end a large tower (and
seemingly two smaller ones also) and chapels projecting on the north
and south (only one of these remains at Ely). It also had a central
tower, and its Lady Chapel was on the north of the choir, as at Ely.

Both the central and the western towers at Bury fell down, the
former in 1210, the other in 1430 : the first was rebuilt, the other
may not have been finished at the Dissolution. One or other contained " the largest bell in England," says a sixteenth-century visitor.

Thanks to the diligence of some monk who was at the pains of
copying down the inscriptions on the windows and paintings in the
church, we know something of its internal decoration. The choir
was surrounded by a stone (?) screen, on the outer side of which
Samson had the story of the Book of Genesis painted in some ninety
scenes. The windows of the south aisle of the nave illustrated the
Life of Christ. The roofs of choir and Lady Chapel were painted
with medallions (like the choir roof at Salisbury). In and near the
choir were more than one representation of King Sweyn being killed
by St. Edmund. Near the high altar stood a great candlestick for
the Paschal candle, made of metal, and having on it (as has the one

at Milan Cathedral) the story of Adam and Eve. Many other works of art, windows, wall-paintings, and hangings are noted by our monk. But a large proportion of them perished in the fire of 1465. That fire, however, spared the shrine of St. Edmund, which stood behind the high altar, and was protected by a massive wooden covering. Our best means of judging of what it looked like is afforded by the pictures in a MS. of Lydgate's *Life of St. Edmund* (Brit. Mus., Harley MS. 2278). It stood on a rich base of marble, green and purple, and was in form like a church without a tower—made of wood, covered with plates of silver gilt, a gold cresting on the top, a gold relief of Christ in glory at the western end, figures in niches along the sides : " Very cumbrous to deface," said Henry VIII's Commissioners. All sorts of offerings of crosses and jewels were hung about it, and four great candles were perpetually alight.

Of all this splendour nothing remains. Only the general form of the church can be traced. The west front, stripped of all its stone facing and built into modern houses, shows relics probably of three portals in the middle. There were anciently bronze doors to the church, an Italian fashion very rare in England, and perhaps due here to Abbot Anselm, who came from Rome. Right and left are two polygonal buildings which once were two-storied chapels. The area of the nave is in private gardens and not accessible ; but the site of the choir may be entered from the Abbey gardens. Portions of the piers which sustained the central tower are left : on one is a modern tablet commemorating the meeting which the barons held in the church when they swore to force Magna Charta from King John. The northern limb of the transept is to be seen ; very little of the Lady Chapel ; fragments of the wall of the apse. The crypt has never been explored : no monastic site in England needs investigation more or, probably, would repay it better. Here it is quite possible that the bones of St. Edmund may rest : when the Commissioners defaced the shrine they would probably not desecrate royal bones ; their master would not approve of that. They might well have buried them decently under the crypt floor.

So much for the church. It is a misfortune that the townspeople were well provided with parish churches ; indeed, the monks, in their anxiety to have their church to themselves, helped to build these churches. Otherwise the nave, at least, of the Abbey church would

BURY ST. EDMUNDS, SUFFOLK: INTERIOR OF ABBEY GATEWAY

have been spared for parochial use. As it is, we have two large parish churches practically in the churchyard, and only rags of the Abbey. Exactly the same is the case at Evesham.

Next, for the principal monastic buildings. These were on the north side of the church : the existence of an earlier cemetery, I suppose, prevented them from being put on the south, as was usual. The cloister garth, about 173 ft. broad, is not accessible, but there is nothing to be seen there. The Chapter House, opening eastwards from the cloister, was a Norman building. It has been excavated, and the tombs of a number of abbots of the twelfth and thirteenth centuries, including Samson, have been revealed and are visible. Adjacent are foundations of which the meaning has not yet been explained. Eastward lay the Infirmary, as yet not found, in the chapel of which four of the earlier abbots were buried. The key to the identification of the Chapter House tombs was furnished to me by a MS. Register of the Benefactors of the Abbey, now at Douai, which describes the order and position of the graves.

The refectory, or frater, was as usual on the side of the cloister farthest from the church (here, the north), and ran parallel with the church. The site is visible, but nothing of detail. Fragments of other structures, perhaps the monks' parlour, nearest to the Chapter House, and another of quite late date down by the river with something like a dovecote, are also to be seen : the abbots' palace was in this part of the precinct.

But it is when we turn from the centre to the circumference that the memorable remains of the Abbey appear. The great space in front of the *Angel*—the *Angel Hill*—is as good a thing as England can show. The upper side is largely composed of very fine brick houses of " Queen Anne " type,[1] and on the lower side is the range of precinct wall and the most magnificent fourteenth-century gatehouse in the country. To the left as you face it, the precinct wall runs on behind the houses and turns a corner towards Eastgate. To the right there soon projects the west front of St. James's Church, and next door to it is the great Norman tower immediately west of the Abbey church ; beyond this some houses, on the line of the walls, and, at the south angle of the precinct, St. Mary's Church. We will shortly examine these buildings. The *Abbey Gate* was built after the great riots of

[1] One of the best, alas ! was burnt in 1929.

1327 ; entering it you will see carved shields which help to date it :
(1) Edward III, (2) Missing, (3) John of Eltham, Edward's brother,
(4) Thomas of Brotherton, his uncle, (5) Edward the Confessor,
(6) Henry of Lancaster, cousin to Edward II.

There was a good deal of imagery on the front : immediately
over the door three niches may have contained St. Edmund and
two archers ; of five larger ones above the central one probably
showed our Lord. The angle-turrets have twelve niches. The

BURY ST. EDMUNDS, SUFFOLK : THE ABBOT'S BRIDGE

detail everywhere is admirable. Passing through it and noting the
extremely fine window on the eastern side you find yourself in the
gardens, which represent the great court of the Abbey. Immediately
on the right the Guest Hall is conjectured ; beyond it the Mint.
On the left, against the precinct wall, a range of offices and stables ;
fronting you was another long range joining on to the claustral
buildings and running right across to the wall. On the slopes beyond
the River Lark, where the School of King Edward VI now stands,
was the Vineyard. Coming out of the Abbey gate again, you may

first turn to the right and follow the precinct wall down Mustow Street and see not only some very good old houses (some have perished of late by street-widening), but the very remarkable structure (13th cent.) called the Abbot's Bridge, where the wall is carried across the river. On the inner side of the wall is space for a footbridge : there were gratings below to prevent access by water.

But very likely (though the Abbot's Bridge must not be missed) you will prefer to turn left on leaving the Abbey gate and look first at St. James's, with its Perpendicular nave and aisles and modern chancel. It serves as the Cathedral church. The west front is very rich, and has the badges of St. James (scrip and staff) and St. John (cup and dragon). Inside I will only notice the one window of old glass in Bury : it is a make-up mainly of two windows, both of early sixteenth century. Below is the Story of Susanna : she is seen with her husband Joachim, and also in the bath, approached by the Elders (in dark purple, with doctors' bonnets), and tried before them. The upper lights have fragments of a fine Jesse-tree with the kings Abia, Asa, Joram, Manasses, and David. In the tracery, *inter alia*, St. Katherine, St. Joachim (father of the Virgin) holding a lamb, and two figures said to be Cain and Abel. All this glass merits particular notice as being of a period little represented in England ; the best example being in the windows of King's College, Cambridge.

Next we come to the Norman tower, as splendid in its way as the Abbey gate : it is of late twelfth century, and serves as the bell tower of St. James's. The great arch once had a sculpture of Christ in glory in its head, but a thoughtful Town Council removed it in 1789 to afford freer passage for loads of hay and straw. Doorways high up on the north and south show where a passage was practicable along the top of the precinct wall and through the tower.

These two gate-towers are unrivalled in their class in England.

Turning into the churchyard, which is a beautiful place, you may see the shapeless ruin of the charnel-chapel, a good view of the north side of St. Mary's with the Notyngham porch, and a fine old house of 1730, once the " Clopton Asylum," now devoted to Church uses. In this churchyard it was that on New Year's Day of 1722 Arundel Coke, barrister, invited his brother-in-law Edward Crispe to take a stroll after supper ; and had a man waiting with a bill-hook, who fell upon Crispe and hacked him and left him for dead. Coke went back to his house and said that Crispe would be in shortly, and spoke more truly than he thought, for soon afterwards Crispe did crawl in covered with blood. He was mended up, and Coke and his accomplice Woodburne were tried under the Coventry Act for slitting Crispe's nose. Coke's defence was that he did not intend to slit Crispe's nose, but to kill him ; and was insistent to know whether the nose could be said to be slit within the meaning of the statute, when the edge of it was not cut through. Lord Chief Justice Sir Peter King was of opinion that it was duly slit, and Coke was hanged.

Then to St. Mary's Church, which is a much finer building than St. James's, though like it in general lines, and contains more of interest. The roofs are admirable. The nave roof is of hammer-beam pattern, with angels, and a long series of saints on the helves (between the windows), mainly apostles and prophets ; towards the west are some virgin saints ; east are the Annunciation (north and south), Edmund (south), Edward the Confessor (north). The aisle roofs have heraldic badges in the spandrels ; the east part of the south aisle over the tomb of John Baret (see below) is painted with his mottoes, *God me guide, Grace me govern*, and others in Latin. The chancel has a wagon roof, the coved cornices painted with angels holding scrolls with the *Te Deum*, and the bosses bearing an interesting variety of grotesques and musician-angels.

The chancel has two large altar tombs with effigies, that on the north of Sir William Carew (1501), the other of Sir Robert Drury (1536). Mary Tudor, widow of Louis XII of France, and then wife of Charles Brandon Duke of Suffolk, removed here from the Abbey, has a modern memorial. The most interesting tomb is that of John Baret, in the south aisle, a "cadaver" in a shroud inscribed *Ecce nunc in pulvere dormio*, with much else, including an English rhyme of some merit. He died in 1467, but his monument was made in his lifetime ; his will, printed in *Bury Wills and Inventories* (Camden Society, 1850), is very long and very interesting.

The north porch, built by John Notyngham, grocer, in 1437, is noteworthy, especially the roof. In this part of the church are some remains of an earlier building, in particular the north door, and the base of the tower. The old aspect of the interior is well shown in a picture (18th cent.) that hangs in the *Angel's* coffee-room.

The other building in Bury which should not be missed is Moyses'

Hall, in the market-place—a Norman house which may have been, like one at Lincoln, a Jew's house, but hardly a synagogue. The front retains fine Norman windows, and a fifteenth-century insertion with a carving of the wolf and St. Edmund's head below it. The lower storey is vaulted. The building serves very rightly as a museum: here may be seen, with much of the material that is familiar, such fragments of decorative sculpture, etc., as excavations on the Abbey site have produced.

Bury is full of good old houses : the Cupola house of 1693 in Meat Market and those on Angel Hill and in Northgate Street being particularly pleasing relics of a time when the county families spent a season in the town. The judicious visitor will no doubt look for the Ladies' School (" Westgate House ") of *Pickwick* : I doubt if he will find it.

On the whole I take Bury to be the most attractive town in Suffolk, perhaps because I know it so well as the shopping-town of my childhood. Therefore I have been prolix.

SOUTH-WEST SUFFOLK

Other things there are in the outskirts which will be noticed as we take the roads in various directions. First we will go south, following the line to Sudbury. There is nothing now to be seen at *Hardwick*, but *Rushbrooke* has a splendid moated house of the Jermyns, and the church, which was fitted with stalls in the collegiate manner by a Colonel Rushbrooke about a hundred years ago, is a curiosity. At *Nowton* the church has a large quantity of foreign glass consisting almost entirely of medallions in yellow stain or enamel, fifty or sixty in number. None is older than the beginning of the sixteenth century, but some are of excellent quality. One rare subject is a scene from the passion of St. Christopher, a red-hot helmet being put on his head.

Hawstead has a fine church full of Drury monuments : an earlier cross-legged effigy is in the chancel. The screen has the sanctus-bell still upon it ; there is an ancient lectern. The north and south doors are Norman. Of the three Bradfields, *Bradfield Combust* is the most interesting ; it was the home of Arthur Young (*d.* 1820), whose tours to inspect the agriculture of England and France are such good reading. The church has wall-paintings : St. George, Christo-

GEDDING HALL, SUFFOLK

pher (and Michael destroyed). At *Gedding* is a beautiful fragment of a moated house, including a splendid gate-tower, ruinous as I remember it, but now in good order. West of the line is *Stanningfield*, where is Coldham Hall, a noteworthy house of 1574, built by a Rookwood, father of Ambrose, the Gunpowder Plot conspirator. The best thing in *Cockfield* Church, which stands well, is a fourteenth-century recess for a tomb. At *Alpheton* is, or was, a St. Christopher wall-painting.

Lavenham will at once attract, and continue to do so. It was a busy place in the fifteenth century, making money by weaving, and in the domains of the De Veres, Earls of Oxford. Two of the principal clothiers, Thomas Spring and Simon Branch, combined with John 13th Earl to build and adorn the splendid church. The chancel is fourteenth century, the nave is fine Perpendicular ; the tower, 140 ft. high, is the most stately in all the county, magnificent plain flint standing on the crest of a gentle slope, and containing a famous peal of eight bells, of which the tenor, dated 1625, and made by Miles Gray, has been called the sweetest in England. There is a fine pinnacle to the staircase turret, north-east of the nave. The nave of six bays is as good Perpendicular as can be seen ; the spandrels of the arcade are richly panelled. The roofs both of nave and aisles have figures on the helves : in the nave apostles, prophets, and virgin saints ; in the south aisle many are grotesque ; in the north they seem to be Old Testament worthies. At the east end are two wooden pews or parcloses or chantries of most remarkable and beautiful work verging on Renaissance, with a good deal of foreign-looking and classical detail. That on the south is of De Vere (Oxford), the other of Spring. The former recalls the carved work in Henry VII's Chapel at Westminster ; but both are very much out of the common. Attached to the chancel on either side is a chapel, that on the north the gift of Simon Branch and Elizabeth his wife, the other (dated 1525) of Thomas and Alice Spring. Each has an inscription on the outside telling of its origin, in a fashion not uncommon in this district.

The chancel itself has a few interesting misericords, one of which shows a crane and pygmy fighting. There are very good screens dividing the chancel from the chapels.

The town has plenty of good ancient buildings, but the former hall of the Guild of Corpus Christi, a splendid timber-framed house, is much the best. A figure carved on the corner post, holding a distaff and the charter of the Guild, is called John de Vere, the founder.

Preston, a little way east, is notable for a very fine porch and, inside, a rich early font and a painting of the arms of Elizabeth, with many symbols. This is a relic of the embellishments of Robert Ryece, author of a *Breviary of Suffolk* (ed. by Lord Francis Hervey, 1902), who put some 167 coats of arms of Suffolk families into the church windows : a few remain.

Proceeding southwards, *Acton* has a famous early brass of 1302 (Sir Robert de Bures), and a later canopied one of Alice de Bryan (1425). And then we come to *Long Melford*, the rival of Lavenham, but perhaps rather richer in interest. The lay-out of the village is most remarkable. At the head of the very long village green stands the church ; below it on the green is the modernized but still picturesque Clopton Hospital ; on your left, as you look

PRESTON, SUFFOLK : FONT

downwards, is Melford Hall, its gardens separated from the road by a broad ditch and venerable wall. The house is of about 1559, with lead-topped turrets. Beyond, the long street with old houses and a water-mill. On the right are avenues leading up to Kentwell Hall, another Elizabethan house. A fragment of yet another, Melford Place, is at the southern end.

The church must occupy most of my space. Its tower is modern, replacing a classical structure with vases on the corners, which I can remember. The original tower fell about 1710. The fabric consists of nave and aisles of ten bays, the Clopton Chapel at the east end of the north aisle ; sanctuary, and eastern Lady Chapel. All that we now see is of the late fifteenth century, and it was built one may say by subscription. Along a great part of the south and north sides and round the Lady Chapel run a series of inscriptions, mainly in English, asking prayers for those who built the several sections (called *arches*) and glazed the windows. The latest date given is that on the Lady Chapel, 1496. Inside, the arcade of the nave is not so fine as that of Lavenham. The great interest here was and is the glass. We have an account of what remained of it in 1688, written by an admirable rector, Dr. Bisbie, printed in Sir William Parker's *History of Melford* (1873), and from this we see that the general scheme of the windows was : on the south side figures of saints and in one case a history (St. John Baptist) with donors' inscriptions below ; on the north a series of portraits or effigies of the Clopton family, their kinsmen and friends ; and, towards the east end, saints. The east window and a few others had been cleared of glass, but over thirty described by Bisbie were more or less complete. Of the greater part of them the eighteenth century made short work. There is now enough left to fill three windows, the east and the two west of the aisles.

In the east window, the tracery lights have heraldry and figures of saints, including St. Osyth carrying her head and a distaff. In the large lights are nine of the portrait-figures and also figures of Our Lady of Pity, St. Peter Martyr (Peter of Milan), St. Edmund, St. Andrew, St. Giles (?). In the west window of the south aisle are ten more portraits, a fine St. Michael, some smaller figures, and some lettering from the Book of Tobit on almsgiving. In the north aisle twelve portrait-figures, a St. Gabriel from the same window as the St. Michael, St. Katherine, a head of St. Christopher, and small kneeling figures, probably donors of the southern windows.

Among the portraits, which are a unique series, those of certain judges and sergeants-at-law are notable for their costumes : Sir William Howard and Richard Pygot are in the east window, John Hough in the south-west. Of the rest, Sir Thomas Montgomerie (east) was eminent, *temp.* Edward IV ; Elizabeth Countess of Oxford (east) ; Thomas Peyton, who built Isleham Church, Cambs. (east) ;

HADLEIGH; TOPESFIELD BRIDGE.

WINGFIELD CASTLE; INTERIOR OF COURTYARD.

John Gedney and Ralph Josselin, Lord Mayors of London (north-west) ; Elizabeth Talbot and Elizabeth Tilney (north-west) may be mentioned. The glass would be greatly improved by rearrangement and clearing out of the modern borders.

In the north aisle is an early alabaster relief of the Adoration of the Magi.

The Clopton Chapel (north-east) has had a great deal of painted decoration, and the cornice retains what I think is unique—a long poem in eight-line stanzas, of which the theme is " Jesu mercy." Seven stanzas remain on the south side, one on west, seven on north ; on the east are five, spoken by Christ. A Litany in Latin is on the central roof beam. The ceiling was blue with gilt stars of lead. An opening on the south into the sanctuary over the tomb of John Clopton has remains of paintings, of Clopton and his family, the risen Christ with scroll *Omnis qui vivit et credit in me non morietur in eternum*, and other scrolls with *memento mori* inscriptions.

In the Martyn Chapel on the south are brasses, and in the chancel a great monument to Sir William Cordell, Speaker and Master of the Rolls (*d.* 1580), who built Melford Hall.

Last, the Lady Chapel. It has a central sanctuary screened off and an ambulatory round it, recalling the arrangement of the Virgin's Chapel in the crypt of Canterbury Cathedral. There are niches for images, now all empty. The building was long used as a school (like that at St. Albans, of which it also reminds one), but is now recovered for the church. Altogether, Melford Church is a wonderful monument of lay munificence. It was very richly equipped with vestments, etc., of which Sir William Parker prints the inventories, and in the same volume may be read a very lively account of some of the Church observances, and a description of images and altars, written after the Reformation by Roger Martyn, a staunch Papist, resembling the *Rites of Durham* on a small scale.

As the Great House at Melford was the scene of the bringing up of Isopel Berners, so *Sudbury*, our next stopping-place, is the Eatanswill where Mr. Pickwick witnessed the election. Sudbury sits very pleasantly in the valley of the Stour, and is dignified by three handsome church towers, of All Saints', St. Gregory, and St. Peter. All three are worth looking into, but in St. Gregory's there is perhaps most of interest. It has the first good font-cover we have encountered, about 12 ft. high, with eight tabernacles for images. Archbishop Simon Sudbury, whom the mob beheaded in 1381, enlarged the church and founded a college adjacent, of which a brick gateway remains. The twenty stalls in the chancel were for the members of this college. The Archbishop's head is in a grated niche in the vestry. Adjoining the south porch on the east is a little chapel of St. Anne, in which a seventeenth-century monument tells in Latin how on a certain day " a camel of Sudbury passed through the eye of a needle " : importing that Mr. Carter, who rests there, was at once rich and virtuous. Here Dowsing exultantly broke down " ten mighty great angels in glass," with seventy other " pictures " : at St. Peter's he destroyed about a hundred, at All Saints' twenty, and thirty brasses.

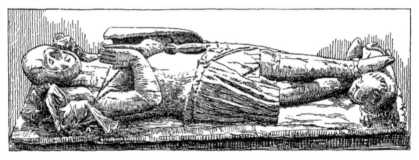

BURES, SUFFOLK : WOODEN EFFIGY

The best ancient house in Sudbury is Salter's Hall, in Stour Street, timber framed, of the fifteenth century ; but a walk about the town will reveal plenty of others. Gainsborough Street has the painter's birth-place. There is nothing instructive to be seen in the remains of the Black Friars' house. The Corporation possesses (or possessed) a fine loving-cup and a fifteenth-century pall.

From Sudbury we may proceed down-stream and make a round, including Hadleigh. The mansion of the Gurdons at *Assington* has a very pleasant Elizabethan front. *Bures*, on the river, is the traditional site of the crowning of St. Edmund, and there is in the parish the ruin of a thirteenth-century chapel to him, which may mark the site, or be simply commemorative. The church, mainly fourteenth century, has a cross-legged wooden effigy. There is a fragment

EAST BERGHOLT, SUFFOLK : THE BELFRY

4

of a beautiful manor-house, and the water-mill and the street make good pictures.

Wissington, or *Wiston*, has a small Norman church with restored apse. It was completely covered with wall-paintings, of which drawings are said to exist : the scanty accounts of them show that they were a very interesting series, probably of the thirteenth century. Only a few fragments were visible when I saw the church.

Nayland on the Stour is a pleasant spot. Jones of Nayland (1726–1800) was a familiar name a hundred years ago : he left a fragrant memory as a pastor and teacher, surviving now perhaps chiefly as the composer of a beautiful hymn tune, St. Stephen's or Nayland. He procured from Canterbury the organ for his church, which stands (or lately stood) in a western gallery. In the church is an altar-piece of the Last Supper by Constable, and there are some panels of the screen, badly painted but interesting. On them are SS. Cuthbert (carrying the head of St. Oswald), Edmund (arrow), Gregory, a king (Henry VI), Edward the Confessor (ring), two defaced kings, St. Thomas of Canterbury. Adjoining the churchyard is a pretty old house.

Stoke-by-Nayland.—The church commands the country-side ; the tower is visible from Harwich. The south door is carved with a Jesse-tree ; other good carved doors are in the district, e.g. at Assington and Polstead. The porch (partly modern) has a vaulted roof. Inside, the tower arch is of fine proportions. The font has the Evangelistic emblems and intermediate figures which demand interpretation. The base and steps are stately. There are brasses and monuments of some interest. Dowsing removed a hundred superstitious pictures here. *Giffords Hall*, in the parish, is a very remarkable fifteenth- to sixteenth-century house, built round a court ; the gatehouse and hall, with minstrels' gallery, are admirable. Facing the entrance is the ruin of a chapel of St. Nicholas (13th cent.). This place was the property of the Mannock family for 300 years.

It is allowable, without trespassing far into East Suffolk, to go across the Roman road (Colchester to Dunwich ?) at *Stratford St. Mary* and take in *East Bergholt*, the birth-place of Constable (1776–1837). Its church has a quantity of fine flint-work : the tower was never finished, and the bells hang in a timber belfry in the church-yard. Flatford Mill, where Constable's father lived, and where he

HADLEIGH, SUFFOLK : THE GUILDHALL

worked for a time (though he was not born in the mill), is always visited.

Turning northward we go towards Hadleigh, via *Little Wenham*. Here is one of the very few small castellated houses of the thirteenth century, with its hall and chapel on the first floor, the chapel with vaulted roof, beautiful window, and a carved figure in the roof. Alterations were made in the sixteenth century (1569 in an inscription over the door), but not in essentials. Of late this unique building has been well cared for ; an early and full account of it is in Turner's *Domestic Architecture*. The church is assigned to the same builder. It has paintings on the east wall—the Virgin and Child, SS. Margaret, Katherine, and Mary Magdalene—and some good brasses and tombs.

Hadleigh is a pleasant small town, with many ancient houses within and about it ; it became rich by cloth-making, but its earliest claim to fame was that here King Guthrum the Dane died (889), and was buried—certainly not in the fourteenth-century tomb in the church, which is called his. Another celebrity is Rowland Taylor, the rector, burnt on Aldham Common under Queen Mary in 1555 ; he has a palimpsest brass in the church (the reverse being of fine Flemish work). The church is very large. Its carved south door should be noted, and also its original two-storied vestry, some bench-ends, and the fragments of old glass collected into a single window. Dowsing had a fair harvest here, taking down thirty pictures and ordering the destruction of seventy more. In almost all cases " pictures " must be taken to mean glass.

The Deanery Tower, to which the rectory house is annexed, is a fine brick gate-tower built by Archdeacon Pykenham in 1495. It was the scene of the " Hadleigh Conference," out of which the Oxford Movement developed. In 1833, when Hugh James Rose was rector, his friends Froude, Palmer, and Perceval met here and discussed the Church situation. The whole story is perhaps best told in Burgon's *Twelve Good Men*. There is a room in the south-east turret of this interesting building which is thought to have been an oratory : it has a brick-vaulted roof and central boss with *Ave Maria*, etc.

Other good old houses are the Guildhall, Hadleigh Hall, Place Farm, Pond Hall.

North-west of Hadleigh is *Kersey*, which with its neighbour *Lindsey* made Kerseymeres and Linsey (or Lilsey) woolseys. Kersey has a beautiful street dipping down sharply to a bottom and rising again sharply to the church. In the street are several groups of excellent small houses, one in particular known as the "Ancient Houses." In the church are some good features : one which I have vainly tried to elucidate is a carved frieze in the north aisle, much broken but illustrating some story. There are many fragments of images, and panels of a screen with kings (St. Edmund) and prophets, besides an eagle lectern, and some remains of a wall-painting of St. George. There is also the P r i o r y (Augustinian). Some massive fragments of ruin stand in the grounds of the farmhouse which occupies the site. They are described as the south aisle of the choir of the church, fragments of tower and transept, and west wall. The kitchen also exists. Little detail is left.

BENCH END AT HADLEIGH, SUFFOLK

Turning s o u t h - west three villages demand a word : *Groton*, a sacred name in Massachusetts, for here was born (1588) John Winthrop, first Governor of the Massachusetts Bay Colony. He is commemorated by a window in the church. *Boxford*, with a pretty stream and mill, and some beautiful timbered houses. The church has a wooden porch (north) of the fourteenth century, with groining ribs of wood, very notable ; the south porch is one of the fine stone and flint ones which are frequent in the region. The Annunciation is in the spandrels here. Both doors are well carved. The font has a fixed cover (17th cent.) opening at the side and painted with texts within. Remains of a wall-painting of a king (Edward the Confessor?) are to be seen, and a little brass of a child, showing him asleep in bed, and inscribed *Dormitorium Jos. Berde* 1606. *Polstead* was the scene of the Red Barn tragedy. In 1827 William Corder deceived and murdered Maria Martin and buried her in the Red Barn (not now extant), representing to her parents that he had taken her away to marry her, and that she was living in the Isle of Wight

CAVENDISH GREEN, SUFFOLK

(or elsewhere). Her stepmother began after some months to dream that she was buried in the barn, and the father and brother made search and found the body. Corder meanwhile had married a respectable woman near London. He suffered at Bury. A play of the Red Barn long held the stage. Polstead Church has Norman work in the nave and tower arch, and a good carved door. When I first saw it in 1881 there was a good west gallery with organ, and high pews painted white, with fragments of the rood-screen worked up into them. Dowsing made a good haul of forty-five pictures : a bit of glass remaining shows that there was a Crucifixion, and there is a fragment of a bishop holding an auger who must be St. Leger.

This ends our excursion to the east of Sudbury. Now turn north-west, up the Stour. Two names of which the sound has gone far encounter us, *Cavendish* and *Clare*. The name of Cavendish is explained by Skeat to mean " Cafa's eddish(-meadow)," *Cafa* being the owner's name, and *eddish* a word still in country use meaning aftermath or second crop. Hence, then, came the great family now Dukes of Devonshire. The church is handsome : in it are two old lecterns, one of wood, the other a brass eagle of the sixteenth century.

Clare takes its name from an Anglo-Saxon called Clare, but it is not an English name, and must be the Latin Clarus : it *gives* its name to the Earls of Clare, the county Clare, Clare College, Cambridge, the dukedom of Clarence, and the Clarencieux king of Arms. Only the merest rags of the building of the Castle (near the station) remain ; but the earthwork on which they stand most likely represents a very ancient fortress, defending a frontier of the East Anglian kingdom.

The church is a spacious town church with western tower and two handsome pinnacles at the junction of nave and chancel,

CAVENDISH, SUFFOLK : LECTERN

which latter is a rebuilding of 1618. Dowsing's exploit here is often quoted, but his memory must not escape a repetition : " At Clare, Jan. the 6th, we brake down 1,000 pictures superstitious ; I brake down 200 : 3 of God the Father and 3 of Christ and the Holy Lamb, and 3 of the Holy Ghost like a Dove with Wings ;

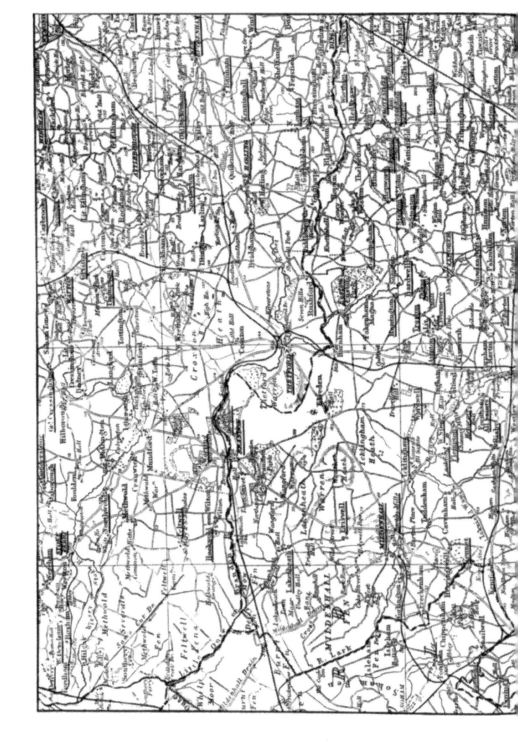

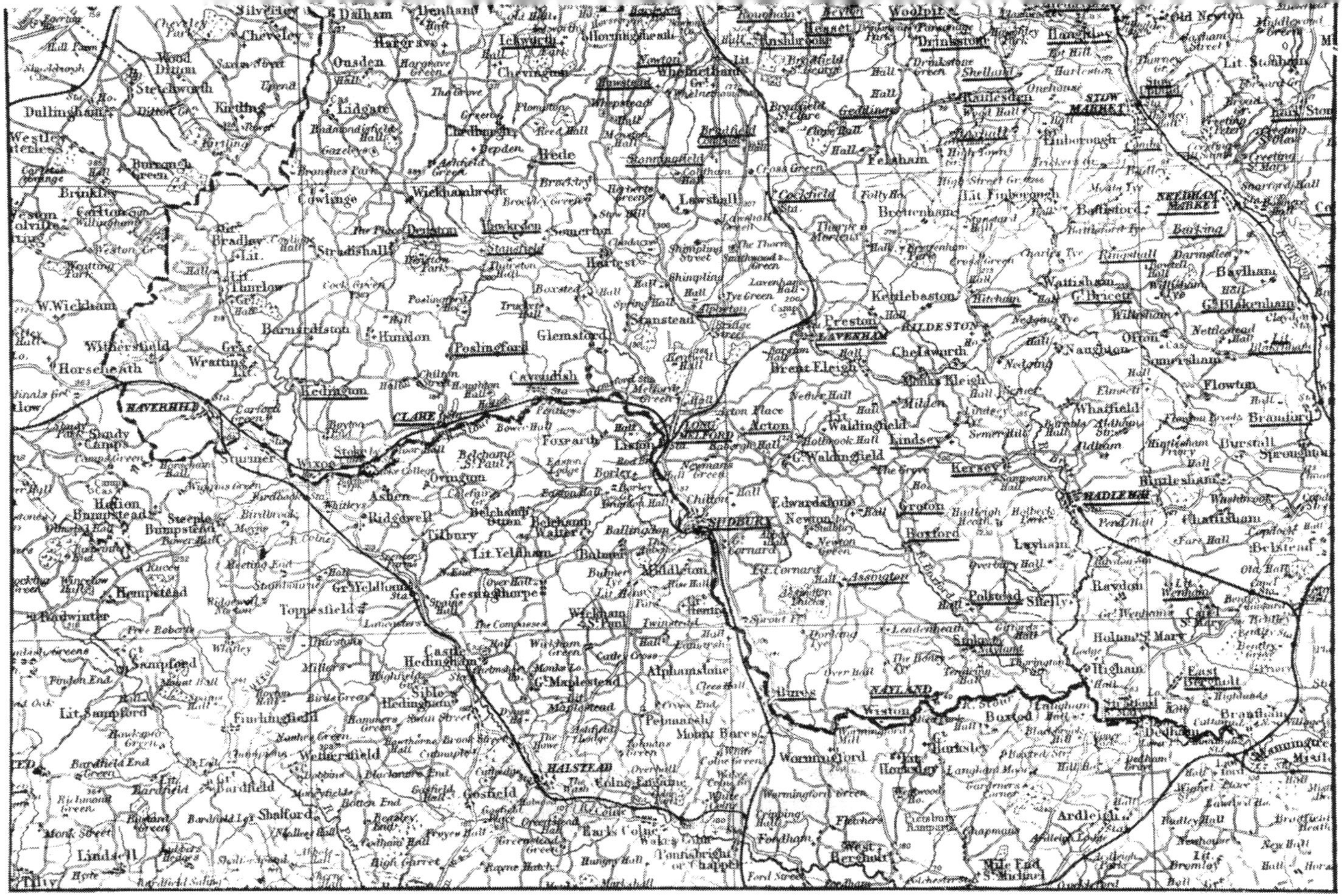

SUFFOLK WEST

SCALE ¼"=1 MILE

and the 12 apostles were carved in wood on the top of the Roof, which we gave orders to take down ; and 20 cherubims to be taken down ; and the Sun and Moon in the east window by the king's arms to be taken down." The Sun and Moon survive, and there was still in the eighteenth century a quantity of heraldic glass. The matrices of brasses are notable here, some of great size, and one large slab to de Godewyk, provincial of the Austin Friars (?) throughout England. There is some screen work and a sixteenth-century eagle lectern. A good house adjoins the churchyard, with fine pargetted front. Note also the sign of the " Swan Inn," a piece of fifteenth-century carving. The market-place and many houses in the town—some with gardens running down to the stream —are charming ; one in particular, in which the great antiquary, Sir W. St. John Hope, lived for some time.

The Priory now makes a beautiful house : some sedilia are the chief relics of the church, but there are also some arches of the cloister, and the infirmary (so-called), a fine buttressed block of buildings to the south-east, is very complete. The remains are mostly of the thirteenth and fourteenth centuries. Here in 1307 was buried Joan of Acre, daughter of Edward I, and wife first of Gilbert of Clare and then of Ralph de Mortimer. A curious prosy poem by one Osbern Sparrow, a brother of the house, is printed in the *Monasticon* and else-where : a dialogue at Joan's grave setting forth the genealogy of the Clares. There are remains of a twelfth-century chapel, now made into a cottage, a short way off the town in the hamlet of Chilton.

Stoke-by-Clare had a religious foundation, originally a Benedictine Priory (at Clare), then removed to Stoke, and in 1415 converted into a Collegiate church with dean and prebendaries, of which (Arch-bishop) Matthew Parker was the last Dean : there is a great mass of documents concerning the college among his MSS. at Corpus Christi College, Cambridge. He rebuilt the nave of the present church, and a curiously small pulpit not later than his time is there : the eastern part belonged to the College. The mansion-house, known as the college, which belongs to the Elwes family (John Elwes the miser was one of Mr. Boffin's heroes), has in it remains of the older Priory buildings : a tower with an inscription is one.

Kedington, which even now I hope retains its old pews, has exceed-ingly fine Barnardiston monuments, screen of 1619, three-decker of

Jacobean style, and a splendid Barnardiston pew—altogether a most pleasing interior. This is my most westerly point.

Turning east we have, at *Poslingford*, an interesting Norman door and some wall-paintings, single figures, one said to be St. Paul, the other holding a square and having a building on his shoulder. A farm-house contains such relics as there are of " Chipley Abbey," once an Austin priory, then annexed to Stoke College. There is nothing of the church, which was cleared away in 1818. *Denston* (Denardiston) Church was collegiate, and is a fine dignified building, with a frieze of large

CLARE, SUFFOLK : SIGN OF THE SWAN INN

running animals along the wall plates of the nave, good screen and stall work with misericords, a tomb with two cadavers in the north chapel, and an east window filled with old glass collected together ; there are a few portrait figures, no saints or scenes. Here is the first of the fonts, of which we shall meet many, with the Seven Sacraments. The order here seems to be (going round from east to north) : Confirmation, Baptism, Marriage, Orders, the Crucifixion, Extreme Unction, Eucharist, Penance. Two houses at least, Denston Hall and the Charity Farm near the church, have portions of mediæval work. At *Hawkedon* there were wall-paintings, and the screen has four saints (James, John, Dorothy (?), and another virgin). Thurston Hall is a fine timbered house. *Stansfield* has a little glass.

NORTH-WEST SUFFOLK

We have now dealt with the southern half of West Suffolk. Returning to Bury we will next examine the north-west quarter. A glance at the map will show the extraordinary contrast between it and any other equal area in the county. The space that is occupied

HAWKEDON, SUFFOLK : THURSTON HALL

by a dozen parishes here would contain twice or even three times as many in the centre or south. It is sandy, open land, subsiding into fen on the north and west, and in summer quite delightful of its kind : anciently by no means destitute of population, as cemeteries at Icklingham, and similar finds, testify. We leave Bury by North-gate, and note on the right the gatehouse of St. Saviour's Hospital, where Humphrey Duke of Gloucester died suddenly in 1446 when about to be tried by Parliament, then sitting at Bury. The belief popular in Shakespeare's time made it a murder : 2 *Henry VI*, Act III, enforces it roundly, and it was a great episode in the splendid Bury Pageant of 1908 ; but neither this view of the death nor, I fear, that which looks on Duke Humphrey as *Good* finds acceptance now. The site of the hospital has been explored, but with no striking result. On the left of the road is the hill which gives its name to the hundred of Thingoe—the Thing-how, the hill of assembly ; and a little farther on at the fork of the Thetford and Fornham roads, on the site of the Franciscan priory of Babwell, is an attractive old house, but not of mediæval date. The Grey Friars came to Bury in 1255, unwelcome neighbours to the monks : twice over they settled in the town and were ejected ; they came to rest at Babwell in 1265. This is in *Fornham All Saints'* parish.

We will confine ourselves now to places west of the road that runs due north to Thetford. *Hengrave* is the first of note, distinguished for its magnificent Henry VIII house, built by Sir Thomas Kytson between 1525 and 1538. The turreted front with mullioned windows, a central portal, above which is a quantity of carven heraldry (Kytson, Cavendish, Davey, etc.), is deservedly famous. Only one quadrangle remains of the formerly larger building. The interior with the bay window of the great hall is most effective. There is much fine panelling in the house, and also some remarkable sixteenth-century foreign glass in the chapel, consisting of twenty-one lights illustrating the Creation, Adam and Eve, the Flood, and Tower of Babel, and the Infancy and Passion of Christ. In common with the rest of the house it has been of late admirably cared for. Hard by the house is the church, long (until 1900) unused for services. It has a round tower, and is full of large monuments of Kytsons and Gages, very stately. There was a St. Christopher wall-painting, and there is some little old glass. I cannot deny myself the pleasure of recording that in the adjacent church of *Flempton* there is or was to be read the epitaph of a former rector named Blastus Godly.

Wordwell, a little north-east, is curious. A tall mound called the Hill of Health with firs growing on it is on the right before the church is reached : there is a large unhewn block of stone upon it, a rare feature in these parts. I do not know whether or when it has been explored. The small church is Norman, with insertions of later windows, etc. Both doors, north and south, have sculptured tympana. That of the south shows a tree in centre and two animals ;

WEST STOW HALL, SUFFOLK

that on the north (inside the church) is extraordinarily rude : I believe it represents the Fall, but there is room for much exercise of fancy. The seats are excellent (? 14th cent.), with animals on the ends, and a frieze on the back of one.

Either coming or going, *West Stow* should be visited, for the beautiful fragment of a great house which belonged to the Croftes family. The turreted brick gatehouse is particularly charming. Inside is a rough wall-painting of the sixteenth century of the ages of man : a boy hawking says, *Thus doe I all the day* ; two lovers, *Thus doe I while*

I may ; an older spectator, *Thus did I when I myght* ; a decrepit senior, *Good Lord, will this world last ever ?* The church has a very pretty angle piscina. West Stow Heath (does the name mean " waste place " as it does in Wycliffe's version ?) has been the scene of many burial-finds of, say, fifth to seventh centuries. The Bury Museum contains much of the results. *Lackford* has a late thirteenth-century font of very fine design carved with foliage.

MILDENHALL, SUFFOLK : MARKET CROSS

Icklingham has two churches, All Saints' and St. James's, the latter much restored, the former containing a good many points of interest— piscinæ, a very beautiful chest (14th cent.), remains of fourteenth-century glass : these consist of canopies, borderings of eagles, and three figures all headless. There are also some encaustic tiles which older books insisted were Roman, but which are plainly mediæval. There are good bench ends in both churches. The discoveries of

Roman remains in the neighbourhood have been very remarkable :
again I refer to the Bury Museum.

Barton Mills has some fourteenth-century glass, figures of SS.
Edmund and John Baptist, and heraldry. It is but a mile from
Mildenhall, which is the most extensive parish in Suffolk, of nearly
17,000 acres, half of which was anciently fen : it includes several
hamlets, Beck Row, West Row, Kenny Hill, etc. I have written
above of the theory which would place Clovesho in or near West
Row. There is a good deal of interest in the large church. The
east window is unique, probably of late thirteenth century, with
seven main lights ; in the head is most elaborate tracery with a
central vesica in which no doubt was a figure of our Lord in majesty.
On the north is a thirteenth-century sacristy with vaulted roof, said
to have been the original chancel. The nave roof (15th cent.) has
its rows of angels, and is very fine ; the aisle roofs are perhaps more
interesting, for they have a variety of carved subjects on the spandrels.
Some of those in the north aisle are : monkey playing the organ,
St. George and Dragon, Baptism of Christ, Angel and Shepherds,
Abraham and Isaac, Annunciation, Michael and Dragon. The
ringers' gallery at the west end is original, and has fan vaulting,
and the north porch with chamber over it is notable. Near the
church is the good old manor-house, where Sir Thomas Hanmer,
Speaker and Shakespearean critic, lived. There is a fifteenth-century
market-cross in the town. Most people who now refer to Mildenhall
speak of it in connexion with the game of golf.

Eriswell lies north, sadly restored, but with a remarkable square
traceried window in the north aisle. There were wall-paintings,
one said to have been of the Miraculous Draught of Fishes,
which I do not believe to have been a subject ever used by the old
painters.

Lakenheath.—The tower is curiously placed rather east of the west
end. The chancel arch, and in essence the chancel, are Norman.
There are wall-paintings in the nave which demand explanation :
they are in several layers, and consequently hard to disentangle. At
the river in this parish there was a horrid scene in 1381 : the king's
justiciar, Sir John Cavendish, was fleeing from the mob, had reached
the bank where a boat was moored, and might have escaped ; but
a woman, seeing him coming, pushed the boat out into the stream ;

FRESSINGFIELD; BENCH ENDS.

FRAMLINGHAM CHURCH.
TOMB OF THOMAS HOWARD, 3RD DUKE OF NORFOLK, AND WIFE.

the mob closed in, and the justiciar was brutally killed. The woman, when the reckoning came, was very properly hanged.

Brandon is famous for the flint-knapping still carried on there, and probably there only, and (perhaps fondly) imagined never to have been disused since the days of flint implements. It is a pleasant place ; the church, over-restored, offers little but the lower part of a rood-screen and some bench ends. Let it not be forgotten that Simon Eyre, Lord Mayor of London, builder of Leadenhall, and hero of the *Shoemakers' Holiday*, was born at Brandon.

Santon Downham, on the very edge of the county, is the end of this excursion. It had its n o t o r i e t y from the great sand floods beginning in 1668, which a south-west wind blew from Lakenheath warren : t h e   o w n e r,   M r. Wright, coped with t h e m   by   planting furze hedges, but years e l a p s e d   before he

STOWLANGTOFT, SUFFOLK :
" THE HARROWING OF HELL "

could reduce the land to stability. Santon Downham is a beautiful remote little place with an interesting church, largely Norman : a curious piece of sculpture over the south door may be a Paschal Lamb ; there is a fourteenth-century screen, and the ivied fifteenth-century tower has a great deal of lettering round the base.

We may return south to Bury by way of Thetford Heath, but of

5

Thetford I will not treat now, only pausing to note that not far from
the Bury road, on the west side, you may catch sight of a block of
stone on the heath which I have always taken to be the base of a
gibbet : certainly the locality would have suited highwaymen.

Next we will take the district north-east of Bury, bounded by the
Thetford line on the west and the Stowmarket on the south, but
leaving over some country near the Haughley-Norwich branch.

HUNSTON, SUFFOLK : PISCINA

We go out of Bury by Eastgate and take the Barton road, noticing
at a corner the scanty ruins of St. Nicholas' Hospital, of which the
only good feature is a pretty window with flowing tracery which was
brought from St. Petronilla's Hospital elsewhere in the town.

Great Barton is best known as the home of the Bunburys, where
Oliver Goldsmith spent happy holidays ; but the house is gone, and
its famous pictures and books dispersed.   The church is handsome,

but offers no special attraction beyond its good nave-roof, and Early English chancel. Barton Mere has an ancient house by it. In the drought of 1868, when the mere dried up, the owner, the Rev. Harry Jones (a pleasant writer), thought he had discovered a lake dwelling. Spearheads, pottery, and bones turned up, but the lake dwelling is questionable.

Pakenham has a central tower with octagonal top, and a good deal of Norman and Early English work. New House is a good Jacobean building. Diverting to *Norton* we find some very remarkable misericord seats in the chancel : one has the Martyrdom of St. Edmund, another that of St. Andrew ; on a third is a pelican and the text *In omni opere memento finis.* There is also glass with some saints, in tracery lights : Christopher, Etheldreda, Andrew, Agatha or Apollonia, and Margaret among them. The font too is rich.

Stowlangtoft should be written Stow Langtoft. The Langtofts were no doubt Normans ; in Normandy their name has become Lintôt (cf. Yvetôt). The church stands rather high, within an ancient earthwork. In its chancel are some fifteenth- to sixteenth-century groups of the Passion and the Harrowing of Hell, of Flemish work. The bench ends, with birds and beasts, are a very complete set, and there are misericords in the chancel. The font has saints about it : Virgin and Child, St. Margaret, Nicholas (?), Peter, Stephen, Paul, George, and (?) John Baptist. Sir Simonds d'Ewes was an " illustration " of Stowlangtoft, and so was a former rector, Samuel Rickards, a friend of Newman.

It is worth while to look into *Hunston* Church, which has south transept and west tower, mainly Early English. Besides the priests' door (south of chancel) and the chancel arch, which are uncommonly good, there is in the transept a double piscina in the angle, and in the east wall a very beautiful niche with foliage border, not unlikely to be overlooked because a modern tablet has been put into it.

We revert to north-west and come to *Ixworth.* The street is full of interest : in particular, near the southern end is a house with some ridge tiles representing figures, of which I do not know the like. Behind the street runs the stream with mill and church and priory on it. The church tower has very fine flint-work devices on the buttresses : the south-east buttress has the name of " Master Robert Schot Abot," who was Abbot of Bury in 1470-3. The tomb of

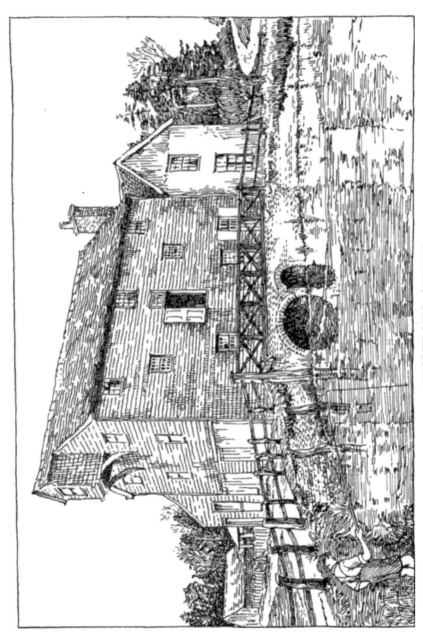

IXWORTH MILL, SUFFOLK

Richard Codrington, north of the altar (1567), is a very pleasing Renaissance work.

The priory is across the stream west of the church. The church was in front of the present house ; its site is marked, and at the front door of the house lie two pigs of the melted lead from its roof which were forgotten by the authorities : they bear the king's seal. A fine vaulted u n d e r c r o f t (12th–13th cents.) is the principal relic of the priory ; the house, most charming in parts, is of later date.

By *Stanton*, which has two churches (All Saints' containing a beautiful ogee tomb-arch), we pass to *Hepworth*. The church was burnt out not many years ago, but the principal curiosity was saved—a very fine font cover, of which the lower stage is surrounded by five castles with men looking out of the doors.

North-west lies *Barn-ingham*, where there is a great deal of good seating, and a screen of some merit. There

HEPWORTH, SUFFOLK : DETAIL OF FONT COVER

is also a puzzle which I will explain, for I have not seen a notice of it : this is a slip of wood fastened to the wall, painted on which in fifteenth-century lettering is : *Flagellatus est ihesus. Sancta trinitas unus deus. Sepultus est ihesus.* It belonged to an altarpiece composed of three Nottingham alabaster tablets representing severally the Scourging, the Trinity, and the Entombment.

North and north-west of this point the country is again open heath and warren, a large space being covered by *Euston Park*, in which John Evelyn's hand may still be traced in the planting of trees, which  he planned for Lord Arlington in 1671. But in the parishes which lie hereabout there is not a great deal for me to describe, though the natural beauties of all this breezy land are great. We will turn south-west, and go to *Bardwell*, which has two attractions, the church and the old Hall. The latter stands on the road south of the village, and shows a beautiful brick front. The church can be seen a long way off. It was beautified and roofed by Sir William Bardwell (*d.* 1434): part of his painting is left on the roof—an angel holds a book with the date 1421. There are por-traitures in two north

IXWORTH THORPE, SUFFOLK : BENCH END

windows, one of Sir William (partly re-stored), others of a knight and lady of the Drury family ; in the tracery is heraldry. Wall-paintings were discovered, drawn, and covered up in 1853 : they are reproduced in the Suffolk Archæological Society's *Transactions* ; they included a St. Chris-topher, legend of St. Katherine, Three Dead and Three Living,

Tree of the Deadly Sins, and Last Judgment. *Ixworth Thorpe* has a series of bench ends with animals and birds.

Honington certainly deserves a visit. The porch is beautiful, the south door Norman ; the font has the Crucifixion. On the south wall is an early painting, quite hard to decipher, but presenting the story of St. Nicholas : we see the wicked landlord and wife killing the three boys who came to their inn, in bed, and St. Nicholas raising them ; on the right is the Martyrdom of St. Thomas of Canterbury. The panels of the painted ceiling have the " *rose en soleil*," the York badge. Robert Bloomfield, the ploughman-poet, was born at Honington. How few of us have read the *Farmer's Boy*, and how surprising it is to learn that it was translated into Latin, Italian, and French, and that 26,000 copies of a seventh edition were sold in or about 1802 !

Troston, where Capel Lofft lived in a small and very beautiful Elizabethan hall, with some excellent plaster ceilings, and where Carlyle visited Buller at the rectory, has another church worth looking at. Here again the porch is excellent ; the screen has suffered from repainting ; window-heads have fragments of nice canopies in the glass, and there are wall-paintings of St. Christopher, St. George and the Dragon (two of this subject, one being, I should say, of the 13th cent.), and the martyrdom of St. Edmund, besides a Majesty or Doom over the chancel arch, not well preserved.

A mile more, and we are at *Great Livermere.* The reader will forgive a little expansiveness here : from 1865 to 1909 the rectory was my home, if not my dwelling-place. The *Concise Description of Bury,* etc. (1827), says : " The Livermeres, for beautiful park scenery, connected with the adjoining parish of Ampton, form the most interesting and delightful spots in the county ; such variety of picturesque views are presented by the winding sheet of water, sloping woods, and scattered venerable oaks and shrubs." The Livermeres and Ampton are in one hand now, Livermere Hall is gone, and many oaks in its park are cut down. " It must needs be that," let us say, changes " come." But village and park have some beauty left. The mere, which extends a mile or more, into Ampton, gives its name to the place ; a name which Skeat says is derived from *læfer,* a flag (cf. Rushmere), and is justified by the growth of flags and bulrushes. It is to some extent an artificial water made in conjunction with the

Ampton owner, probably about 1800. *Great Livermere* Church is on the eastern edge of the park : it has a Decorated nave with beautiful tracery in the windows ; the chancel was probably thirteenth century. The screen, which is exceptionally good in design, is late fourteenth century, the chancel roof has some admirable carving, and there are

HONINGTON, SUFFOLK : FONT PANEL, " THE CRUCIFIXION "

massive old seats of merit with fleur-de-lys ends. In the north-west corner is a fourteenth-century wall-painting of two kings, perhaps part of the Three Dead, etc., and in the south-east of the nave is a Christ appearing to Mary Magdalene. The tower has been beheaded ; the nave is thatched.

Little Livermere Church stands alone in the park : the village, which once surrounded it, was removed outside the park in the course of beautification. The tower was heightened in order to be visible from the Hall ; the interior was made lovely with a ghostly imitation of vaulting in plaster, and a parlour pew faces the three-decker. All this very characteristic furnishing I hope survives. The church is inconveniently placed and little used. It was, I believe, a quite early building. In the north wall (the only original wall) is a blocked flat-headed doorway with some very primitive ornament. Arundel Coke, of whom we have heard above, was thought to be buried half inside and half outside the churchyard wall, on the east. A large unworked stone under a tree by the churchyard gate affords matter for speculation : the only other that I have seen in the district is that on the Hill of Health at Wordwell.

Ampton, whose park joins Livermere, is another pretty village with old almshouses, old school-house, and small church ; from its north wall projects a chantry (converted to a squire's pew) which has the inscription over it : *Capella perpetue cantarie Johannis Coket*—the date is 1483. Arthur Young is most eloquent about the beauties of Ampton and Livermere, nor am I confident he errs.

EASTWARD, THE STOWMARKET AND EYE DISTRICT

We have now to leave Bury for good, along the Stowmarket line, east and south-east.

Rougham Common has provided some very remarkable antiquities from tumuli : two burials of the Roman period were found in brick chambers—one of these chambers is still preserved *in situ*, and there is a model in the Bury Museum. The church is very handsome, with a hammer-beam roof and angels ; the helve-figures are mostly headless, but the fact that one holds a boat (St. Jude) and others have scrolls, indicates apostles and prophets. A little glass remains : pelicans, Virgin and Child, King with Sceptre.

The church of *Thurston*, north of the line, has been largely rebuilt, after the fall of the tower ; but there are numerous fragments of old glass, and the font and some seats are good. *Beyton* Green and village are picturesque, but *Hessett* claims careful attention. The church stands very prettily in a well-kept churchyard, in which is more than one mediæval tombstone. Tower and aisles are fifteenth century, and have parapets and flint-work : on the tower are initials J. B. (for John Bacon ?). A south porch, with St. George and Dragon in the spandrels of the door, may be an addition. The north aisle has an external inscription in flint-work to say that John and Katherine Hoo built a chapel, battlemented the aisle and heightened the vestry

HESSETT, SUFFOLK : BACK OF BENCH

(which is mediæval). The chancel is fourteenth century, the east window showing very unusual tracery. Inside, the font has an inscribed base to Robert and Agnes Hoo. There is a repainted screen and good seating ; but the exceptional features are wall-paintings and glass. Of paintings : in the south aisle a figure said to be holding a church, but uncertain—some reckon him as Christopher ; farther east a Virgin and Child, with a text painted over it, used to be visible ; in the north aisle is a double painting of interest—the upper part a Tree of the Deadly Sins, hell mouth at bottom and two devils. The lower left branch has Avarice with two bags, the upper left Greed (*Gula*) drinking, at top is Pride, on right Anger with sword, and below him probably Envy. These trees are not very uncommon: one was at Bardwell. The lower part represents Christ surrounded by all manner of tools and implements : sword, shears, hammer, scythe-blade, cart-wheel, spoon, gridiron, harrow, shovel, pitch-fork, jug or dice-box, and, most noticeable, a playing-card, the six of diamonds (black). The meaning of these paintings is undetermined ; they occur, e.g., at Lanivet (Cornwall), Ampney St. Mary (Glouc.), Michaelchurch-Eskley (Heref.), Skenfrith (Mon.) : sometimes known as " Christ of the Trades." Prof. E. W. Tristram sees in them the influence of *Piers Plowman* ; they show Christ sanctifying labour. Another explanation which seems to me plausible is that they show the injuries inflicted on Christ by the sins of all manner of people. Here the juxtaposition with the Deadly Sins and the presence of the playing-card may be significant.

Glass : in the east window of the south aisle are two figures which are always misunderstood because a bishop's head has been fitted on to one. They are the two Maries, the mother of James and the mother of Simon, Judas, Joses, and James, etc., with their children. On left the children are James with scallop and John with cup, on right they have boat, string of coins (?), loaves, and club. The windows in the south wall are all fragmentary ; the third from the east has relics of a Last Judgment, the fourth St. Paul and part of a Trinity. In the north aisle one had the story of St. Katherine : two scenes remain—her trial before the emperor, and the burning of the fifty philosophers whom she converted. In the next two were prob-ably the joys and sorrows of the Virgin : parts of Betrayal, Presenta-tion, Annunciation (twice), Scourging, Resurrection, are visible. I pass over smaller fragments. The church possesses two rarities— a painted linen burse to keep hosts in, the Veronica-face of Christ and the Evangelistic emblems on one side, the Paschal Lamb on the other ; and a cloth (really lace-work), perhaps for covering the pyx. They have often figured in exhibitions of church art. The village street here is pretty : note the brick pillar carrying the sign of the inn.

Tostock has some good benches and *Drinkstone* an elaborate screen. *Woolpit* is not without celebrity. In the twelfth century two green

children came up out of the ground in harvest time (as is related by
William of Newburgh), and said they lived underground in St.
Martin's land (query Merlin's), and had heard the bells ringing up
above and suddenly found themselves in the field. Their own land
had churches in it, but the light was dim like twilight : across a
broad river there was a brighter land. These underground people

were detained by those who
found them. The boy soon
died, but the girl lived and
married a man at Lynn. More
prosaic is the discovery here of
earth which made fine white
brick, Woolpit brick. Many
good old mansions were dis-
astrously faced with it. About
1820 " the Emperor of Russia
had a small quantity sent over
for him to look at." Of the
church, the spire fell in 1852,
and was rebuilt. The south
porch is rich and beautiful.
The nave-roof is double hammer-beam, with angels and
helve-figures, eleven on a side :
Christ and some apostles are
distinguishable. The aisle-
roofs also have angels and
helve-figures. Over the chancel
arch is a beautiful and unusual
canopy in wood. The screen
has had new saints painted on
the panels ; but it is worth
recording that years ago St. John Baptist and St. Edmund (first
and second on south) were decipherable. The eagle lectern is old
and good : it is said to have a trap-door in the tail to extract
contributions put in at the beak. There are also good bench ends.
Not far from the church (on the east) is a Lady's Well, once a goal
of pilgrims, still not without repute for healing.

WOOLPIT, SUFFOLK : LECTERN

Elmswell tower and porch are rich in flint-work : wheels, lily-pots and sacred monograms. *Wetherden* has had a very fine double hammer-beam roof, but seemingly all the angels and helve-figures are new. The need for this we owe to Dowsing, whose entry is : " We brake down 100 superstitious pictures in Sir Edward Silliard's (Sulyard's) aisle, and gave order to break down 60 more and to take down 68 cherubims." At *Haughley* is a great castle-mound, and the Hall is of 1557. Here is a junction from which you can go north, south, east, and west ; but *Stowmarket* makes the better centre. It has a pleasant street and old inns. The church is mainly fourteenth century, with some interesting circular windows (north-west). A l a s ! the old organ, a Father Smith instrument once at Walsall, was swallowed up in 1870 in a new one. In the grounds of the former vicarage is a Milton mulberry tree; for Thomas Y o u n g , once Milton's tutor, was long vicar here. In *Stowupland* parish is a very pretty moated house, Columbyne Hall, now a farm.

COMBS, SUFFOLK : BENCH END

Next door to Stowmarket is *Combs*. The church is remote from the village, but the key is now to be had at the one house near it. The chancel has some beautiful fourteenth-century windows, and screens and benches are good ; but the glass is more noteworthy.

It is said to have suffered by an explosion of Stowmarket powder mills in 1871. As it is of unusual type I shall give some details. Remnants of three sets of subjects, collected into the south aisle windows, are distinguishable, viz. :

(1) The Works of Mercy, Ministering to the Thirsty : a lady by a house pours out water and a man gives it to a beggar ; inscriptions in English :

> I am thrysty ful drye y wysse
> Haue her drynke thy for hym y^t doth . . .

Feeding the Hungry : man and woman give bread :

> For mete ye I hungre . . .
> Brodyr haue mete anow y^t . . . .

(2) Story of St. Margaret. Five scenes are left, very much out of order : the probable sequence is :

(a) She is keeping sheep : the persecutor Olybrius rides up ;

(b) She is brought before a king : a demon-idol on a pedestal ;

(c) She is thrust into a portcullised gateway, with an iron collar and chain on her neck ;

(d) In prison the devil, a dragon, swallows her : she emerges, and (on right) birches the devil ;

(e) She is about to step into a cauldron of oil or pitch.

(3) A genealogy of Christ : a number of names and figures of kings and ancestors survive : Ozias, Ezechias, Manasses, Josias ; Nacor, Aram, Aminadab, Naason, Salmon, Booz, Obez (sic) ; Jesse, David, Solomon, Asa ; Abraham, Isaac, Jacob ; Adoth, Mathan Eliud, Amon (many are wrongly labelled rex). A scene of Baptism performed by a bishop : a dove comes on a ray from right ; the mother and child are nimbed, the father is in ermine. Evidently this belongs to the life of a saint, probably of noble birth. The genealogy is very much scattered : something would be gained here by rearrangement.

We will next deal with a district along the line north and north-east of Stowmarket. *Bacton* has a Last Judgment painting in the usual place over the chancel arch, and a screen at the west end : *Cotton*, mostly a fourteenth-century church, an angel-roof, and some noteworthy remains of glass ; in south aisle four figures belonging to a

EYE, SUFFOLK

79

series of prophets (14th cent.)—*Micheas* and *Abdias* have their names,
another holds an organ ; at the east end of the aisle a figure of Christ
(headless) ; in the clerestory angels in the heads of the windows (15th
cent.). *Gipping* also has some glass in the east window, a Mary and
John from a crucifixion, an abbot, a knight and lady. *Mendlesham*
has a handsome church, with good flint-work ; but I doubt if I should
mention it, were it not that Camden or his editors have mixed it up
with Rendlesham, and said that King Redwald's crown, weighing
60 oz., was found in both places.

Gislingham, somewhat north-west, has glass : on it the columbine
flower ; fragments which seem to belong to a Crucifixion scene ;
a St. Katherine and another, and a Coronation of the Virgin. The
porch is inscribed : the builders were Robert and Rose Chapman.
The brick tower is of 1635. *Burgate* and *Mellis* should not be omitted.
At the former is the very fine tomb and brass of Sir William de Burgate
(1409), and also a late fourteenth-century chest with remains of a
painting of a knight. The towerless church of *Mellis* has some not
despicable glass of six-winged angels.

Going farther north-west we have the two *Rickinghalls*, Superior
and Inferior, of which the Inferior has the better church : round
tower with octagonal top, a good deal of Early English work, and
two windows with really beautiful tracery, in the southern and
eastern parts. *Botesdale* was important in the coaching days, and has
a pretty street. It had no proper church, but a chapel of St. Botolph,
which joins on to a house, formerly a school endowed by Sir Nicholas
Bacon (1576) ; *Redgrave* was its mother parish, and here lived not only
Sir Nicholas, but another great lawyer, Sir John Holt (*d.* 1710), and
both their very stately tombs are in the church, which also has an
exceptionally fine fourteenth-century east window of seven lights.
We are now close to the Waveney and the Norfolk border. Turning
east we come to *Wortham*, where there is a curiosity in the shape of
the tremendously massive but roofless and gutted round tower of the
church, said to have been a watch-tower for the Abbot of Bury's
men : fire-places are pointed out, but seem to have no flues. *Pal-
grave* has a Norman font and some armour.

Of *Hoxne* and its connexion, real or supposed, with St. Edmund
I have written. In its handsome church wall-paintings were found
in 1835, and uncovered again recently. One of them is a Tree

BURGATE; BRASS OF
SIR WILLIAM DE BURGATE AND WIFE, 1409.

of the Deadly Sins; here the tree is surmounted by a figure of a
man with a sceptre (who may be Pride), and the trunk of it is
being sawn through by two devils. Another is of the Works of
Mercy, not all legible. As in some other cases it is a woman
who is doing the charitable acts. A third is curious and difficult:
said to be the Last Judgment, which is generally over the chancel
arch, not, as here, on the north wall. To me it looked like a
picture of the Lamb on Mount Sion surrounded by a multitude
of figures ; but I own that this is a very unusual subject. There is
also a large figure (? St. Michael) in the north-west angle. A
Maynard tomb of 1742 sculptured by Stanley is very good of its
kind. The font has figures.

This shall be our farthest point north-east for the present: we
return south-west to *Eye*. I have spoken of its Red Book, which once
was at the Priory. The site of that Priory has been lately investigated,
and the plan of the church determined (see *Antiquaries' Journal*, 1927).
There is hardly anything above ground, but the church was proved
to have been exactly on the lines of the original mother church of
the Abbey of Bernay in Normandy, with three eastern apses and
apsidal chapels on the very short transepts. The parish church has
excellent features : the tower is of the handsomest, and the flint-work
good. The rood-screen is, so far, our best painted screen : the
figures on it must be named, running from south : (1) effaced, probably St. Peter to answer to St. Paul at the other end ; (2) St. Cecilia
(not Agnes or Agatha), a sword in her throat, and roses at her waist ;
(3) St. Blaise ; (4) St. Lucy, knife, and book with her eyes on it ; (5)
St. William of Norwich holding a cross and nails ; (6) St. Katherine,
sword, book, and wheel ; (7) St. John Evangelist. North side : (8)
St. Edward the Confessor ; (9) St. Agnes, sword in throat, and lamb ;
(10) St. Barbara, palm and tower ; (11) St. Dorothy, basket of
flowers ; (12) Henry VI ; (13) St. Ursula, arrow, and virgins under
her cloak ; (14) St. Edmund (?), arrow ; (15) St. Helena, cross ;
(16) St. Paul. (14 is otherwise called Christina.) A very pretty
timbered house adjoins the churchyard. *Brome*, north of Eye, retains
only a fragment of the old Cornwallis mansion with a tower ; but it
is worth noting that the gardens have been a great nursery for learners
of the topiary art, the fashioning of yews into birds, and many other
strange forms.

6

Yaxley Church, west of Eye, has screen panels with delicate patterned gesso ground, of SS. Ursula, Katherine, Mary Magdalen, Barbara, Dorothy, and Cecilia, and a Doom in wall-painting over the chancel arch. There are considerable remains of old glass collected into the east window, including a St. John and fragments of a Passion. A " Sexton's Wheel " is at the west end. Excellent porch, flint-work, and niche for image on the tower.

A few places on either side of the line to Needham Market shall be gathered up. On the west *Buxhall* has an east window (14th cent.), so beautiful as to have got into the *Glossary of Architecture*, and some glass (14th cent.), especially in the south windows. On the north possibly a Coronation of the Virgin, and fragments of a Creed. *Shelland* (west), a donative, has a seventeenth-century chapel dedicated to Charles the Martyr.

Rattlesden, farther west, has an imposing church with double hammer-beam roof to the nave, the angels mostly modern. The base of the screen had SS. John of Beverley (not common), Dorothy, Magdalen, Edward the Confessor, and doubtless others—all probably indecipherable now. Flint-work is good, and font pretty. Farther south I select *Hitcham, Ringshall*, and *Great Bricett*. *Hitcham* has a fine fourteenth-century church with added clerestory and hammer-beam roof. There have been wall-paintings, and a screen with angels holding instruments of the Passion ; also bench ends, and a porch restored in memory of the excellent botanist Prof. Henslow, who was long rector. *Ringshall*, rather remote, has over the south door a

YAXLEY, SUFFOLK : HOUR-GLASS

painting of the Works of Mercy (early 14th cent. ?) in compartments. On left is a large half-length figure of Christ, then pairs of figures of which the decipherment is not very easy ; Nos. 1–3 will be. the hungry, thirsty, naked ; 4 is the stranger ; 5, which should be the prisoner, is gone ; 6 seems to be the sick man lying on his back ; 7 is certainly burial. The chancel roof is pretty.

Great Bricett.—Here was an alien priory of which the mother church was unusually far away, being Nobiliac, now S. Léonard, in the Limoges district. The priory church survives ; it is a long towerless building joined at the west end to the Manor-house. Excavations made here by Mr. Fairweather in 1926 showed that the east end was formerly apsidal, and that there were two transeptal chapels also with apses. The beautiful four-teenth-century east window is a restoration : glass of the four Evange-lists (14th cent.), now in a south window, comes from it. The south door is Norman, and the jamb has inscribed stones on which the name *Leonardus* can be read (and in spite of repeated efforts I could never read any more : the stones are not in order). A west arch, visible only from the Manor-house, is Norman.

RATTLESDEN, SUFFOLK : POPEY HEAD

On the other (east) side of the line, *Earl Stonham,* is a church with transepts (there was once a central tower), without aisles, but with a clerestory, which has a curious effect. It has one of the finest of the hammer-beam roofs : pendants alternate with angels holding shields—the helve-figures (twenty-two) are headless. Wall-paintings exist of the Last Judgment (over chancel arch) and St. George (in south transept). Others of which there are records and very

ERWARTON HALL AND GATEWAY, SUFFOLK

faint traces were : on east wall of south transept, a Martyrdom of St. Thomas of Canterbury, said to have been converted into a Martyrdom of St. Katherine ; and in the north transept the Magi journeying and adoring, the Angel and Shepherds, and Nativity. At *Stonham Aspall* the top storey of the tower is a glorious wooden erection of 1743. The clerestory was pinnacled. Besides good bench ends there is glass (14th cent.), heraldry, and a Jesse-tree (west of north aisle) on ruby ground.

Crowfield Chapel has a wooden chancel which is picturesque, and near it is a fine pigeon-house of 1731. *Needham Market* has a delightful old street and mills on the river. Its church has a good roof and a pierced buttress. At *Barking*, which is handsome, are curious patterns of grape-vines in relief about the windows. Something like these is in the Renaissance chapel, now a dairy, of the old Bacon mansion at *Shrubland*. This house has famous gardens laid out on a steep slope by Barry, and some primeval Spanish chestnut trees. *Coddenham*, hard by it, is a very pretty village. In the church is a curious alabaster of the Crucifixion with the swooning Virgin, Angels with chalices, and the Centurion. The roof is excellent, and there are some screen panels of the prophets dated 1534. *Great Blakenham* offers a pretty wooden porch with an image ; *Little Blakenham* some wall-paintings spoilt by retouching ; *Claydon* the beautiful front of Mockbeggars' Hall. At *Bramford* are beautiful parapets on the north side, and a rarity in the shape of a *stone* rood-screen of three arches (14th cent.).

EAST SUFFOLK

So we come to *Ipswich*, the capital of the county. But of Ipswich it is not my intention to say much. Its numerous churches contain on the whole very few curiosities. Some late painted panels at St. Matthew's show St. Leger holding his auger, though possibly he may be meant for St. Erasmus : men and women members of a guild kneel to him. The font at the same church has on it the Five Joys of the Virgin and the Baptism of Christ.

The *Ancient House* will be visited, and the museum, now housed in the mansion of Christchurch, which Felix Cobbold saved and gave to the town. It contains some few MSS. which came from Bury

WINGFIELD CASTLE, SUFFOLK

Abbey. Nor will the thought of Mr. Pickwick, Mr. Nupkins, and Mr. Grummer be far from the mind of the intelligent visitor.

On the tongue of land which lies between the estuaries of the Orwell and Stour, *Erwarton* is worth a visit for the mediæval tombs in the church of the Davillers family : one cross-legged effigy, effigies of knight and lady, and of a lady (13th and 14th cents.). Also for its Hall (of about 1575), which has a rather later brick entrance lodge of the most eccentric kind, running up into chimney-like pinnacles.

On both banks of the Orwell are pleasant parks and houses : *Wherstead, Freston, Woolverstone* on the right, *Orwell* and *Broke Hall* on the left. The sixteenth-century brick tower that stands in Freston Park reminds one of the "high lonely tower" of *Il Pensieroso :* it may have been, like that, a place for recluse study, or a look-out. It is attributed to one William Latimer. On the left bank are the meagre remains of the small priory of *Alnesbourne* and the pretty walk known as Gainsborough's Lane, which he frequented and painted.

In the area between Orwell and Deben there are few remarkable spots, but one very much frequented place, *Felixstowe*, anciently called Filstow, or even I fear Filthstow ; but I hasten to say that no depreciation was intended by the name : it is believed to mean a place of felled trees. The Felix part has crept in from a neighbouring priory of Walton St. Felix. So Professor Skeat.

Now to examine the county north of Ipswich : a great many parishes have to be passed *sub silentio*, and the first I stop at is *Helmingham*, the home of the Tollemaches. The house is splendid, surrounded by a moat (with one practicable drawbridge and one permanent bridge), and itself surrounding a court. In the fine hall is armour removed from the church ; in the library are many treasures, the chief being the Lauderdale MS. of Alfred's translation of Orosius, a copy coeval with Alfred. The park has great old oaks ; the country round was one of the later haunts of the Great Bustard. The tradition that Queen Elizabeth stayed here in 1581 and that her lute is here is discredited. The church is full of Tollemache monuments, one so lofty that a dormer in the roof has had to be built for its top.

Near *Debenham* is another exceedingly picturesque moated house, Crows Hall, now a farmhouse. Its avenue and some old adjacent buildings called the Barracks are delightful.

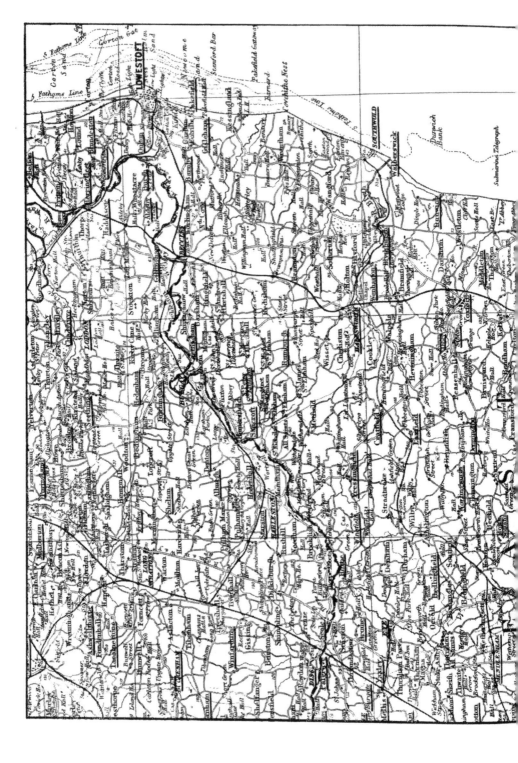

SUFFOLK EAST

Worlingworth is handsome ; besides flint-work, bench ends, and some little glass, it has a very exceptional font-cover about 20 ft. high, formerly rich in images which are all gone. The constant tradition is that font and cover both came from Bury Abbey. It has been asked what a monks' church could want with a font, but it is clear enough from records that the Abbey church had a baptistery of some kind at the south-west. What the evidence is for the Bury origin of this beautiful cover I do not know, but it is well worth seeing.

Redlingfield has the curious little church of a Benedictine nunnery. The old parish stocks are to be seen in the vestry : not many specimens are left in Suffolk—I shall note a few more. *Wingfield* has one of our rather rare castles, a four-sided moated building with gatehouse and angle-towers. On the west side a Tudor house replaces the original structure. One drawbridge remains. This was the castle of the de la Poles. Michael de la Pole built it in and after 1384, after marrying the Wingfield heiress. The court is practically empty of any buildings. The church was made collegiate by Sir John Wingfield (*d.* 1360), and probably only the tower of the present building is older than that. In it are admirable monuments of Sir John Wingfield, Duke John de la Pole and his wife (with tilting-helmet above), and Michael de la Pole and his wife with wooden effigies originally coloured. There are good parclose screens to the chapels of St. Margaret (north) and Our Lady (south). The Trinity Chapel (north-east) is the vestry, and has a room over it.

WINGFIELD CHURCH, SUFFOLK: JOHN DE LA POLE, DUKE OF SUFFOLK, AND WIFE,
ELIZABETH PLANTAGENET

The college buildings were replaced by a farmhouse south of the church ; there was originally a quadrangle. A most careful history of Wingfield was published in 1926 by the Rev. S. W. H. Aldwell, the Vicar.

Turning east we come to *Fressingfield*, where Archbishop Sancroft, after his deprivation for not taking the oaths to William and Mary, lived and died (1693) ; he had played his part well under James II, and he was a very learned and virtuous person, but I fear his old age was rather sour and peevish. The church here, and two others on the homeward route (for we are now going south), *Cratfield* and *Laxfield*, are very rich in fine woodwork, especially bench ends. *Laxfield*, although it was the home of William Dowsing, has kept its font with the Seven Sacraments and a screen, now at the west end. It also has a pretty timbered Guildhall. *Cratfield*, too, has a Seven Sacrament font and an old " Town House."

But of *Fressingfield* a word more must be said, for according to Dr. Cox (*Bench-ends in English Churches*) this church " is better fitted throughout with excellent fifteenth-century benches than any other church in the kingdom." This is high praise, but deserved. The fronts and backs of the seats are patterned ; especially noteworthy

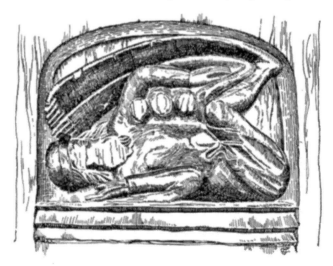

DENNINGTON, SUFFOLK : " SCIAPUS "

are two towards the west end.   One, known as the Passion Bench,
has a series of shields bearing emblems of the Passion, viz. the cock ;
the buffeting hand, and a jug ; the IHC ; the pillar, scourges, and
cords ; the cross, crown of thorns, and nails ; the reed and sponge,
and lance, in saltire ; the ladders, pincers, and hammers ; the seam-
less robe, and three dice on a board.   Next to this is another bench

FRAMLINGHAM, SUFFOLK : ENTRANCE TO THE CASTLE

with devices appropriate to SS. Peter, Paul, and Andrew.   Many of
the popeys are admirable.[1]

   At *Dennington* there is again a great wealth of woodwork : at the
east end of each aisle a chapel is screened off with beautiful parcloses
(coloured in modern times).   A carving of a Sciapus on a bench end

---

[1] At *Wilby* are notable remains of glass, and some wall-painting, which I have not seen.

does not escape notice ; he lies on his back and holds his huge foot (or feet, but there should be but one) over him to shade him from the sun. Such men were to be found, if not in Africa, then somewhere else. In the chancel there is unusual figure-carving in stone at the end of the string-course, of an apostle, and some grotesques. The fine tomb of Lord Bardolph (1441) has alabaster effigies of him and his wife. The old glass, not inconsiderable in amount, is decorative only, without pictures. The modern glazing is absolutely vile.

Framlingham has the largest castle and one of the most interesting

FRAMLINGHAM CHURCH : " THE ARK."   DETAIL OF TOMB OF HENRY FITZROY,
DUKE OF RICHMOND

churches in the county. The castle stands very beautifully overlooking a flat, and now consists of an irregular area surrounded by a wall and thirteen towers. Some brick chimneys, added in Henry VII's time by Thomas Howard, Duke of Norfolk, are a pretty feature. In a modern hall within the enclosure is the organ gallery from the church, which ought never to have been displaced. It was to this castle that Mary came shortly after Edward VI's death—in a very troubled time—and here the county declared for her. The fate of the castle was on the whole kind : it was sold in 1635 to Sir Robert Hitcham, and he bequeathed it to the Master and Fellows of Pembroke

College, Cambridge, who still own it.   He directed that the interior buildings should be pulled down.

The church, a large one, has a very late chancel, built to contain Howard and Mowbray tombs, some of which were removed hither from Thetford Priory Church at the Dissolution.   Six shall be noticed : (1) South of altar, Thomas Howard, 3rd Duke (*d.* 1554), and his wife ; round it are images of Christ and the Apostles.   (2) North of altar, Henry Fitzroy, Duke of Richmond (*d.* 1536) ; on this is a frieze of twelve Old Testament subjects, a very unusual thing : they are (i) Creation of Beasts and of Eve ; (ii) Adam and Eve led by God into Eden ; (iii) the Fall, the serpent human-headed ; (iv) the Expulsion ; (v) the Beginning of Toil ; (vi) Cain and Abel ; the Sacrifices and the Murder ; (vii) the Ark and the Drunkenness of Noah ; (ix) Abraham and the Angels ; (x) Lot flees from Sodom : his wife is seen as a pillar with human head ; (xi) Sacrifice of Isaac ; (xii) Giving of the Law : the Golden Calf.   (3) North-east, the two wives of Thomas Howard, 4th Duke.   (4) Beside this, Elizabeth his daughter.   (5) Henry Howard, Earl of Surrey, the poet (*d.* 1547), and his wife : this dates from 1614.   (6) South of altar, Sir Robert Hitcham (*d.* 1636).   Another beautiful thing in this church is the organ case, which came from Pembroke College Chapel in 1707. Mr. Andrew Freeman, in his book *English Organ Cases*, dates it about 1580 : it was repaired in 1674 by Thomas.   Nailed to the back of it is a front of another early organ, also very handsome.   In order to produce its right effect this organ ought to stand in a western gallery, as indeed it did in my recollection, but it is now down on the floor. There is an obscure wall-painting on the north wall.   The modern glazing is almost as bad as that of Dennington.

Parham, to the south, has a fair church : the stocks lie in the tower. It also has Parham Old Hall, a most picturesque moated house of the Willoughbys, where Crabbe used to stay.   But I must here record an outrage.   Down to 1926 there stood over one of the entrances to the premises a very beautiful stone arch of late fifteenth century, on which were carved five shields of Willoughbys and their alliances.   The work was wonderfully sharp and good ; and standing where it did, in the hedge-row, the gateway was as unexpected and pretty a thing as one could wish to see.   In 1926 an American, whom I cannot qualify politely, prevailed on the owner to sell it and removed it. Language fails me when I think of it forming the portal perhaps of the stately Buggins home in — no., on — Plutoria Avenue, Zenith City, flanked, it may be, by Assyrian bas-reliefs and surmounted by a mosaic from Sicily. For we may be con-

fident that our purchaser is a man of widé art-sympathies, and as he might probably say himself, a whale for culture.

To the west are *Monk Soham* and *Earl Soham*, the former the home of Archdeacon Groome, a friend of Edward Fitzgerald. F. H. Groome's book, *Two Suffolk Friends*, gives an admirable sketch of the man. The font here is curious. At *Earl Soham* mediæval verse inscriptions on the tower are to be seen, and a good roof.

SOUTH-EAST SUFFOLK

We will next attack the country on the east and take in the sea-

WOODBRIDGE, SUFFOLK : THE STEELYARD

coast, using the Lowestoft line and road as the backbone.

Between Ipswich and *Woodbridge* the flaming red lion on the good old inn of *Martlesham* arrests attention, and originates a simile " red as Martlesham lion " ; probably it is a figure-head, put up here

ERWARTON CHURCH; DAVILLERS TOMB.

about 1750. *Woodbridge*, on the Deben, presents a delightful aspect, especially from the river : the tall church tower is seen at its best. Inside, the church has something to show : a font with Sacraments and Crucifixion, and the remains of a screen. The figures on this have been replaced by new painting, but the originals of many panels are on the north and south walls. There was an inscription asking prayers for John and Agnes Albrede, the makers, " crucis crucifixi " and " tocius candilbeem." The ancient panels are of SS. Dorothy, Ursula, a Bishop, Simon, Matthias or Matthew, James the Less, Andrew, James the Great, John Bartholomew, Philip, Jude, Thomas, a Bishop ; also there is record of SS. Edward, Kenelm, and Oswald, who are on the new screen.

The Seckford Charity, endowed with lands in Clerkenwell, has been of the greatest benefit to Woodbridge, supporting a school, hospital, and other institutions. It was left by Thomas Seckford in 1587. Seckford Hall is an imposing Elizabethan house, and the Shire Hall and a number of other good old houses give character to the town. Edward Fitzgerald was much at Woodbridge : his proper home was Boulge (north-west), and there he lies.

Ufford has a church full of interest in a pretty village. The stocks stand outside the churchyard gate ; the porch is a good specimen. The famous thing in the church is the font cover, a really magnificent mass of tabernacle work surmounted by a pelican. The lower panels of the screen remain, and have rather poor paintings (on south) : (1) Sancta Agnes ; (2) St. Cecilia ; (3) St. Agatha ; (4) St. Fides ; (5) St. Brigida ; (6) St. Florentia—this last a martyr of the neighbourhood of Beziers, perhaps. Bench ends, which are very good, include besides beasts and birds SS. Katherine and Margaret. There is painting on the nave-roof, and a cornice of angels in the chancel. On the north wall was a painting called of St. Christopher, but really, I believe, of St. John Baptist. Relics of glass there were, but on a recent visit some had disappeared. Notably in a south-east window : two angels with unusual scrolls—(1) " With sancte dominaciones shall wise emperors and kinges be " ; (2) " With virtues shall holy prestes and religious be crowned and rewarded "—which is similar to matter in the *Golden Legend*.

It is pleasant to find that Dowsing occasionally met with some resistance in the discharge of his loathsome work. He paid two

7

visits to Ufford ; on the second occasion he is unwontedly diffuse.
After telling us what he broke down (among other things " We brake
down the organ cases and gave them to the Poor "—generous creature!),
he says : " There is a glorious " (by which he means not handsome but
pretentious) " cover over the font like a Pope's tripple crown with a
Pelican on the top picking its breast, all gilt over with gold.   And we
were kept out of the church above 2 hours, and neither Church-

UFFORD, SUFFOLK : THE CHURCH AND STOCKS

wardens, William Brown nor Roger Small, that were enjoined these
things above three months afore, had not done them in May, and I
sent one of them to see it done, and they would not let him have the
key.   And now neither the Churchwardens nor William Brown nor
the Constable James Tokelove and William Gardener the Sexton
would not let us have the key in 2 hours' time.   New churchwardens,
Thomas Stanard, Thomas Stroud.   And Samuel Canham of the
same town said : ' I sent men to rifle the church,' and Will. Brown,
old Churchwarden, said : ' I went about to pull down the church,
and had carried away part of the church.' "   William Brown's attitude

ORFORD CASTLE, SUFFOLK

long puzzled me, but I have come to see that he and Canham were speaking of Dowsing !

The area between Deben and Alde, bounded by the sea, contains some very attractive, breezy, heathy country, and some few sites of interest. On the road that leads south to the mouth of the Deben is *Sutton*, where we saw reason to think that St. Edmund was first buried after his martyrdom, and that the battle which he lost was on the tract called Staverton Forest or Park : there is no house, but the forest is said never to have been disturbed. Sutton Church has a font with figures, including two of the Annunciation. Those round the base are said to be servers at Mass. *Ramsholt* tower, a round one with buttresses, has been called Roman, but for no good reason : its position is effective. *Alderton* has an epitaph pleasing for its candour, which I must quote in part : it is that of the Rev. Robert Biggs, forty years rector (*d.* 1769) : " He was not distinguished for his Activity or literary Abilities. But he was what is more truly valuable—An honest Man."

Near the centre of this area is *Butley*, where one relic of the fairly rich Augustinian Priory, founded in 1171 by Ranulph de Glanville, is specially remarkable. This is the gatehouse, till lately the par-sonage, now in private hands. The passage through is built up and forms a fine vaulted room ; the bases of former towers at each side also have vaulted rooms. Over the gateway is a great piece of heraldic ornament in the shape of thirty-five coats-of-arms (Vere, Beauchamp, Bohun, Plantagenet, etc.), arranged in five rows of seven apiece ; there is also much beautiful flint-work of traceried windows, and a triplet of niches at top ; all this of the fourteenth century. On the south gable is a wheel-window imitated in flint-work, from which perhaps the modern one over the Ethelbert Gate at Norwich was adapted. The remains of the chief buildings of the Priory, not very considerable, are in farm buildings a little way off.

Orford—village (or town, for it had Mayor and Corporation and two members), castle, and church—is fascinating. Of the castle (1165) the late Norman keep alone remains. In it is a very pretty Norman chapel. The building recalls Hedingham and Castle Rising, and was copied, it is said, at Conisborough ; it is divided into three main floors. Recently it has been generously presented to the nation by Sir Arthur Churchman, and appeal is being made for a fund for its

ORFORD CHURCH, SUFFOLK : CHOIR ARCADE

repair and upkeep. The destruction of the outer buildings must have been comparatively recent ; a rough view drawn by John Norden in 1600 shows a pretty complete enceinte.

Of the church the eastern part was Norman : there were transepts, of which the east wall of the north transept is to be seen in the north aisle. The choir arcade stands in part, roofless and ruined ; the columns, some of them, are decorated with raised spirals in a very rare fashion. The western part of the church, now in use, has lost the greater part of its tower. The mouldings of the west and south doors and of the nave arcade are admirable. The font is rich : it has the Evangelistic emblems, a Pietà, and an " Italian " Trinity (the Father supporting the crucified Son before Him). There is some really fine woodwork of 1712 now in the chancel ; there *was* a rather nice organ case given in 1790 by Lord Orford. Brasses are numerous.

A merman was caught at Orford in the thirteenth century, and kept for some time : he could not be induced to take an interest in the services of the church, nor indeed to speak ; eventually he escaped. The authority is Ralph of Coggeshall.

The evolutions of the River Alde are surprising. Below Snape Bridge it rapidly widens, and just south of Aldeburgh comes within 100 yards of the sea, from which it is only parted by a shingle bank. Then it turns abruptly south, and runs along just inside the shore, and in passing Orford becomes the Ore. The marshes and flats about it have a peculiar attraction. One more place is to be mentioned in this area, and that is *Iken,* on the south bank of the Alde. There is nothing very remarkable about the church, but its position and the view over the Alde are curiously delightful. Moreover, somewhere here was Ikanho, the monastery founded by St. Botolph, of whom I have said something already.

Returning to the Woodbridge-Aldeburgh road we come, about *Snape*, into a continuation of the heathy region where the gorse in spring is wonderful. At *Snape* there was a priory, but not much is left of it : the font in the church is good. *Aldeburgh*, " sung " by Crabbe and figuring in Wilkie Collins's *No Name*, has a special charm for those who, like myself, have known it from childhood ; but I do not find it easy to put that charm into words. There was formerly a great deal more of Aldeburgh : the beautiful Moot Hall must once

SNAPE, SUFFOLK : FONT

103

have stood in the middle of the town, and not, as now, on the brink of the sea. In front of one or other of the shallow seat recesses at the base stood the town stocks. The church is dignified and spacious, but does not contain any special curiosities. The martello tower at the south end is worth walking to for the view of sea and river and marsh. Not far north is *Leiston* Abbey, Premonstratensian. The remains are considerable, partly in and about farm buildings. Like Butley, it was founded by Ranulph de Glanville (in 1183) on a site nearer the sea ; in 1363 the house was transferred to the present site, so all the buildings are of late fourteenth century. However, some portions were removed and re-used. In *Archæologia*, Vol. 73, Mr. A. W. Clapham gives an excellent plan of the abbey. A chapel on the north of the choir has been roofed, and is used for services when retreats are held here. The church was cruciform with oblong chapels east of the short transepts. The plan of the whole is traceable, the cloister garth, chapter-house on east, refectory on south. One pretty detail is a sculptured cross-head, with the Crucifixion and the Virgin and Child, to be seen in the chancel ; another is part of an early sixteenth-century gatehouse in brick, which was added on the west side.

MID-EAST SUFFOLK

We proceed north, taking stock of a broadish band of country. *Saxmundham* is a pretty little town with good houses. *Yoxford* is the " Garden of Suffolk." Just west of it is *Sibton*, our only Cistercian Abbey. The ruins consist of the south side of the church giving on the cloister area, and remains of some of the surrounding buildings ; it might be well if they were cleared of ivy. *Middleton*, east of Yoxford, has a St. Christopher wall-painting ; and on the coast is *Dunwich*. How much of this once populous city with " fifty-two churches " is left at this moment I will not undertake to say ; but the shell of All Saints' Church, the two gateways of the Franciscan Convent, and the Norman apse of St. James's Hospital Chapel were there not long ago. In its time it was a bishop's see and a rich port : early in the fourteenth century the harbour was destroyed and 400 houses went. By 1550 four churches had gone, and destruction was not to be stayed : a great storm in 1740 dealt frightful havoc.

Blythburgh Church was a very sumptuous one ; after a long period of decay it has been repaired and cared for. Externally the aisle parapets are fine, with pinnacles surmounted by figures, two of which represent Christ and the Virgin, the others being demoniac or symbolic of vices. Under the east window is a series of crowned letters which I do not think have been rightly interpreted as yet, though a solution has been offered. The clerestory also seems to have been pinnacled, or meant to be. Inside, the roof was once full of coats-of-arms of benefactors (?). There is a great deal of good carved work : the stall fronts have figures in high relief of the apostles, Stephen, John Baptist, Christ, and the Virgin. As is traditional in East Anglia, Philip has three loaves, and Jude a boat : Simon should have a fish, but here has a " T " cross. There is an ancient lectern, and there are some very remarkable bench-end figures which illustrated, some of them, the occupations of the months (reaping, the vintage, sowing, killing a pig, warming the feet, holding a flower, tying up faggots), the Works of Mercy (a man in bed, and a man sitting in the stocks with his hands chained down and a collar on his neck), the Deadly Sins (Gula, hands on stomach). The glass, of which there must have been a great deal, is now chiefly confined to small figures of

BLYTHBURGH, SUFFOLK : BENCH-END CARVING OF MAN IN THE STOCKS

saints in tracery lights : popes (Stephen, Eleutherius, Paul, Marcus); bishops (Felix), Apostles, St. Katherine and (?) Barbara. An old Jack of the clock, dated 1682, remains. Of the priory near the church the remains are negligible. *Walberswick*, a haunt of artists, had also a very large church. The tower and a part of the south aisle remain, the rest is in ruin.

BLYTHBURGH, SUFFOLK : STOUP

West of Blythburgh is *Wenhaston*, known for its curious painting of the Last Judgment, on boards which filled the top of the chancel arch : it is a late work, but out of the common.

East is *Southwold*. Its fine church of St. Edmund has perhaps the richest screen, in respect of its paintings, that we have yet come upon. It extends across nave and aisles. In the north aisle the paintings are of the Orders of Angels, in the centre of Apostles, in the south of Prophets. A list may be given, running from north :

I. (1) Angel with shield of the Trinity ; (2) Gawbriel ; (3) Michael Arkeangelus ; (4) Potestates holding devil in chain ; (5) Dominaciones with chalice and host ; (6) Cherubyn, six-winged, on wheel ; (7) Sarafyn, similar, but red ; (8) Troni holding ciborium ; (9) Principatus standing in a tower ; (10) Virtutes (lettered Principatus) holding vessel of fire ; (11) Angelus with souls in a cloth ; (12) Angel with shield of the Church.

II. (1) Philip with loaves ; (2) Simon (or Matthew) with scimitar ; (3) James the Less with club ; (4) Thomas with spear ; (5) Andrew ; (6) Peter ; (7) Paul ; (8) John ; (9) James the Great ; (10) Bartholomew ; (11) Jude with boat ; (12) Matthew with halbert (or Simon with oar).

III. (1) Baruch ; (2) Osee ; (3) Naum ; (4) Jeremias ; (5) (Helyas) ; (6) Moses ; (7) David ; (8–12) names mostly gone— Isaiah, Amos, *Jonas*, Ezekiel.

In these paintings note the beautiful delicately diapered grounds in the apostle-section. The faces were repainted by G. Richmond, R.A.

The woodwork between choir and aisles, a chest with St. George and the Dragon, and a Jack of the Clock, are all to be marked. Out- side over the west window is *Sancte Edmunde ora pro nobis* in crowned letters. The stocks stand near the yard gate.

We will now turn inland and look at a district as yet unvisited. *Westhall* is the first stop. The church here has some elaborate Norman work at the end of the south aisle, visible inside : a wall-arcade is above the west door. This aisle was originally the nave. The tower has been added at this part, and conceals the old vestry outside.

The font is most remarkable : it has the Seven Sacraments and the Baptism of Christ (broken but recognizable). The order of subjects is : south-west—(1) Baptism ; (2) Orders : the book in the deacon's hand was inscribed ; (3) Baptism of Christ : Angel on left with gold robe ; east—(4) Eucharist ; (5) Extreme Unction ; (6) Penance, with Angel and retreating devil ; (7) Marriage ; (8) Confirmation. Traces of colour are copious. But besides this, on the pilasters separating the faces are minute reliefs (in gesso ?) of figures under crocketed canopies, very delicate.

WESTHALL, SUFFOLK : PANEL OF FONT—" PENANCE "

Painted screen panels remain, of rather rough work, but worth enumerating : from north—(1) James the Great ; (2) Leonard, book and fetter ; (3) Michael ; (4) Clement, pope with anchor ; (5) Moses ; (6) Christ as transfigured, with gold face ; (7) Elias ; (8) Anthony, hog and bell ; (9) Etheldreda ; (10) Sitha with rosary ;

(11) Angnes (Agnes), sword in throat, and lamb ; (12) "Beda" for Brida (?), crowned abbess with book and chain ; (13) Katherine ; (14) Dorothy ; (15) Margaret ; (16) Apollonia with pincers and tooth. The cornice is inscribed : Thomas Felton and Margaret Alen, widow, are named.

Glass remains in the heads of the fourteenth-century chancel windows ; it is good decorative work.

There are traces of wall-paintings (in splays of windows and on south wall), but nothing decipherable. A brass in the south aisle gives a very long genealogy of Nicholas Bohun (1602).

Some ancient stones worked into a credence table in the handsome church at *Halesworth* (a market town) may be worth a look ; the old rectory and other houses are pretty. *Rumburgh* (north-west) had a small priory dissolved by Wolsey for the endowment of his Ipswich college ; the base of the church tower is a massive piece of Early English building. We then find ourselves among the grouped parishes, the *Ilketshalls* and the *South Elmhams*. There are four Ilketshalls and seven South Elmhams, one of them (St. Mary's) being more commonly known as Homersfield. In *South Elmham St. Cross* (or Sancroft St. George) is the ruin known as the Old Minster, which Harrod, the Norfolk antiquary, claimed as the cathedral of the Elmham bishops. It stands in an enclosure said to be Roman, and undoubtedly shows the plan of an early type of church with apse and western narthex. But the researches of Messrs. Clapham and Godfrey at North Elmham (in Norfolk), for which see the *Antiquaries' Journal* of 1926, have demonstrated the existence of a more important early church there, and those who still have a hankering after the Suffolk Elmham would suggest either that the S. Elmham Church was abandoned owing to Viking raids, or else never finished, or that the bishop may have been allowed to have an alternative cathedral church. At *South Elmham St. Peter* are the very attractive remains of a moated manor-house of the fifteenth century, once the abode of the Tasburghs.

Two pleasant towns on the Waveney, *Bungay* and *Beccles*, now come into view. *Mettingham*, east of Bungay, had, like Wingfield, its four-teenth-century castle and college, the latter originally founded at Raveningham in Norfolk, but moved in 1393 to the castle. The founder of both was Sir John de Norwich (*d.* 1361). A good deal remains of the castle walls, the gatehouse being the most interesting

feature. The college was inside the enclosure. The church has a good
Norman north door. At *Bungay* the remains of Bigod's castle are perhaps the characteristic thing ; at *Beccles* the distant view of the town
from the Norfolk side, and the church. This has a detached bell-
tower, never finished, of great massiveness, and two porches with very
beautiful flint-work : in the roof of one is a boss with the Assumption
of the Virgin. The churchyard, sloping away to the river, reminds
me of that of East Dereham. Roos Hall is a fine Elizabethan house
or fragment.

NORTH-EAST SUFFOLK

There remains the little peak of Suffolk which lies between the
Waveney and the sea, and ends at Yarmouth. We will go round it
and come back by Lowestoft.

Leaving Beccles we go east to *North Cove*. Here the wall-paintings
are earlier than usual, of late thirteenth century. They take some
deciphering, but I believe the following note of them, taken in 1884,
is correct :

North of chancel a vine pattern : Entry into Jerusalem. Bearing
the Cross (below). Nailing to the Cross. Deposition (below). The
Last Supper. Below, the Crucifixion, obscured.

After a window we have—The Resurrection. The Harrowing of
Hell. A vine pattern.

South side : The Ascension, larger figures. The Last Judgment.
Christ on the rainbow between the Virgin and John Baptist, full-
length Angels on either side hold the Cross and lance. Below
Christ's feet Angels blow trumpets. Twelve people rise : the coffin
lids are very conspicuous ; angels welcome the blessed and drive away
the lost.

Barnby, a curious narrow church, also has paintings, on the south
wall, viz. : the Crucifixion with the thieves and the piercing of the
side. Three figures in the splay of a window : uncertain. The
Works of Mercy ; in centre a full-length figure of Christ. The works
are, on left : Visiting two men sitting in the stocks, Visiting the
Sick, Clothing the Naked, below Christ's feet, Burying the Dead.
On right : Feeding the Hungry, Giving Drink to the Thirsty, Taking
in the Stranger. There is, or was, also a St. Christopher.

Turning up by *Oulton*, where is some Norman work in a central tower, and by Oulton Broad, where George Borrow died, we get to *Somerleyton*. In the rebuilt church is the old painted screen which has on it (from left) SS. Michael, Edmund, William of Norwich with hammer, Laurence, someone with a saw (?), Thomas of Canterbury, Anne and the Virgin, Andrew, John, Magdalene, a bishop, Sitha with key and book, Stephen, Dorothy, Edward the Confessor, and George with a wreath on his head. Over the south door is a bit of sculpture with the Evangelistic emblems.

Herringfleet, an odd little round-towered church, where parsons are never instituted, has an east window filled with foreign glass of late date : a few pieces are English mediæval. In a south window are two figures of the fourteenth century—Helena (?) with long cross, and Katherine.

Of St. Olave's Priory—the owner is still called Prior—there is little left.

Fritton is remarkable. The chancel, lower than the nave, is apsidal and vaulted. From its east window is said to have come a head now in the east window of Herringfleet Church. The restored screen with wheel-work tracery is early ; there is a St. Christopher on the north wall. We are now in a land of lakes and decoys, among which that of Fritton is famous.

Belton has wall-paintings : the Three Dead and Three Living has been retouched. Certain figures on the left do not seem to belong to this scene. Below it appear the legs and fish of a St. Christopher. There is also a picture of St. James the Great.

From Belton we diverge to *Burgh Castle*, the best Roman building which Suffolk has to show, and one of the best in all England, where Roman buildings are apt to be rather unimpressive. This fort, which is probably Gariannonum (observe the likeness of Gari- and Yare), dominates Waveney, where it becomes Yare, and finely over-looks the flat. The plan is rectangular, but there is no wall on the west. There are rounded bastions, six in number ; the walls run to about 14 ft. in height and are 9 ft. thick. In this place, as I have said, St. Fursey is thought to have built his monastery in the seventh century. Not a great deal has been found within the area, which measures 640 by 413 ft.

Hence it is obvious to go east to Yarmouth, which I shall not touch at present, and then turn south along the coast. *Gorleston*, really a

FLATFORD BRIDGE, SUFFOLK

DENNINGTON CHURCH; EFFIGIES OF WILLIAM, LORD BARDOLF, AND WIFE.

SWAN HALL; STANSFIELD.

suburb of Yarmouth, had a church of some interest. But you will read a very misleading account of its riches in most books about Suffolk. Someone whom I cannot identify thought well a hundred years or so ago to pick out of Dowsing's *Journal* a long paragraph full of phrases, enumerating images and pictures destroyed—and then to say that all this havoc was wrought at Gorleston by a deputy of Dowsing called Jessop. The thing is an absolute forgery, as anyone can ascertain who is at the pains to read White's edition of *Dowsing* (where it is quoted as true), and mark down the several clauses. The church had a number of paintings on its north wall, but this was rebuilt in 1872. There is still a painting (of the Trinity) in a tomb canopy. At Gorleston Priory it seems that at the beginning of the fourteenth century there were some extraordinarily skilful artists : a group of lovely psalters came from there, of which one—the Gorleston Psalter—now belongs to Mr. Perrins of Malvern, while the finest of all, which was at Douai in the town library, was buried during the War, and hopelessly spoilt by damp. Those who would pursue the subject can find it admirably treated in Eric Millar's *English Illuminated MSS.*, ii.

Blundeston has two literary associations : one with Gray, who used to stay with Norton Nicholls at the Lodge here, the other, of course, with *David Copperfield*, born and bred in the Rookery, and paying his visits to Daniel Peggotty from here, conveyed by Barkis. The Rookery is identified with the Rectory, but this is not satisfactory : neither the Rectory nor any still extant house commands the church-yard as directly as David's home did.

The church has a curiously small tall round tower, which may have belonged to an earlier building, part of which, e.g. the south doorway jambs, survives. On the screen are painted angels ; on the north side some have scrolls : Passio Christi Salu(atoris ?).

Of the many modern attractions of *Lowestoft* I need not speak. The name means Hlothuwig's toft, and tells of a dim Ludwig or Louis. The old church, remote from the town, is large and dignified : it contains a good brass eagle, a font with pairs of figures on the bowl, much broken, and the matrix of a brass of a good old man, Thomas Scrope, a Carmelite, bishop of Dromore in Ireland (*d.* 1491)—he wrote books about his Order, led a very ascetic life, and died at the age of 100.

Pakefield, just south of Lowestoft, has been terribly eaten into by the sea. Its church is a double one : it served two parishes and had

8

two rectors till 1748. It really consists of two churches placed side by side. The brass of John and Agnes Bowf (1417) has a good epitaph in English rhyme. Portions of a painted screen remain ; some were worked into a reredos. A very faint St. Christopher had, or has, the inscription :

(Christophori Sancti speciem quicunque tuetur)
Illa nempe die nullo languore gravetur.

There is a chalice of 1337.

Gisleham has a round tower with octagonal upper storey. In the splays of two windows on the north side are paintings of crowned angels half length, and below them figures (one wearing a wreath) whom I cannot identify. The arrangement is unfamiliar. Some of the books tell of painted panels of a screen, but these I did not find. There is an early blocked north door.

Thus ends a very rapid survey of Suffolk, in which about one in every three parishes is noticed. The churches have been the staple ; of houses a good many have found mention, but there are plenty of others—small, old moated mansions occupied as farms—which might well have been included. I have said nothing at all of the large halls of more modern date.

ARMS ATTRIBUTED TO
ST. EDMUND, KING AND MARTYR.

BINHAM PRIORY; DETAIL OF WEST FRONT.

NORFOLK

In dealing with the larger county of Norfolk I can hardly hope to escape the censure of those who know the land and its literature. Both are large and full of matter. Nor, though I have seen much myself, can I claim direct knowledge of all that I describe.

It has been a question difficult of decision where to begin : whether to link up with Suffolk by one of the various roads on the southern border, and, if so, by which. After much hesitation I have settled to plunge *in medias res*, and begin with—

NORWICH

Norwich is as full of historic interest as any city in England ; it compares, one may say, with London, York, and Bristol in regard of its ancient commercial and ecclesiastical importance, and in the great number of its urban parishes.

It cannot be expected that a complete guide should be incorporated in this book, and it would be tiresome to give only outlines which are bloodless. I shall therefore presuppose that my readers will consult some other guide-book (there are several good ones), and shall proceed to tell them what I think they ought not to miss.

First of course comes the cathedral. The East Anglian bishopric, after having been located at Elmham (see above), was moved to Thetford about 1070 and to Norwich in 1091. The present church was begun in 1096.

All the main parts of it are Norman, that is to say, the nave, transepts, choir, central tower (not spire), and the two apsidal chapels projecting from the main apse. The principal additions to the nucleus have been the spire (1361), the clerestory of the choir (14th cent.), and the Bauchun (wrongly called Beauchamp) Chapel on the south (14th cent.) ; besides all the stone-vaulted roofs (15th and 16th cent.). It must also be noted that at the extreme east end there used to be a Lady Chapel. The original Norman one, which was apsidal, was replaced by a beautiful Early English one in the thirteenth century, the work of Bishop Suffield. This perished in the sixteenth century (under Dean Gardiner, it is said), and only the fine arches that led into it remain. Outside, the west front is mean and horribly refaced, and the south transept is yet more dismal in aspect. But the rich Norman central tower, the spire (total height 315 ft.), and the upper stage of the choir with those flying buttresses which we so seldom see in England, are all delightful. Inside, you will probably notice at once that the choir projects into the nave, or in other words, the stone screen (which bears the organ) is placed *west* of the transept ; and you may recollect that this is also the case at Westminster Abbey. It was in fact the normal arrangement in churches to which a monastery was attached ; but it has not survived in many.

A short digression here. It is, broadly speaking, true to say that nowhere but in England were monasteries attached to cathedral churches. Normally there was a Bishop, and the cathedral was manned by a Dean and a body of Canons who were not monks : they are said to be " seculars " not " regulars." Examples of such cathedrals in England are York, London, Lincoln, and Salisbury. But in England many of the great cathedrals were served by monks, who lived in a monastery adjoining the church. In these cases the Bishop was nominally the Abbot, but he had little to do with the monastery : it was governed by a Prior, who for all practical purposes was the Abbot. Examples of such cathedrals are Canterbury, Winchester, Norwich, and Ely. Now when the Reformation came and all monasteries were dissolved, it became necessary to reconstitute these monastic cathedrals, and they were all assimilated to one form, and put under Deans and Canons. And the cathedrals that were so reconstituted are said to be (irrespective of their age) of the *New Foundation*.[1] So, while York is of the Old Foundation, Canterbury is of the New.

So also is Norwich, and its choir is arranged for monks to worship in ; for monks wanted more space for their own use, and liked to have more of their church shut off from the public than Canons did. Another notable feature at Norwich is the ancient bishop's throne, restored in recent years, which stands in the central arch of the apse behind the high altar, facing westwards. This recalls the most

---

[1] Of course Henry VIII also created some quite new bishoprics, e.g. Peterborough and Oxford.

NORWICH CATHEDRAL: SOUTH AMBULATORY

ancient practice. Of the furniture of the choir the brass lectern and the stall-canopies (15th cent.), surmounting seats with very notable misericords (14th cent.), are the great features ; nor, though it is a work of the nineteenth century, would I deny some praise to the organ case. It is at any rate a comfort to have it in its proper place on the screen. The lower part of the screen is the ancient *pulpitum* of stone : in it were two little chapels, of St. William, the boy martyr (so called), and of Our Lady of Pity. I have written of St. William in an introductory chapter.

In the choir aisles are two very remarkable pieces of ancient English painting (in which, by the way, Norwich is rather rich). In the north aisle on the vaulting of the Relic Chamber are some very fine late thirteenth-century figures. Each of the four divisions had three : (1) Three Virgins—SS. Mary, Katherine, and Margaret ; (2) Three Apostles—SS. Peter (as pope), Paul, and Andrew ; (3) Three Martyrs—SS. Stephen, Edmund, and Thomas of Canterbury ; (4) Three Confessors—SS. Martin, Nicholas, and Richard of Chichester.

In the south aisle is a retable or altar piece of late fourteenth century, which is one of the most beautiful that has survived. It came to light in 1847. It had been somewhat reduced in size, turned face downwards, and used as a table in one of the vestries. It is in five compartments, representing the Scourging, Bearing the Cross, Crucifixion, Resurrection, and Ascension. The third or central panel may have been somewhat taller than the rest : the head, shoulders, and arms of the crucified figure have been sawn off. Part of the frame remains, bearing shields which have been assigned to Norfolk families (Despencer, Morieux, Howard, etc.). The background of the scenes is in gilt gesso, with most beautiful patterns in relief, such as we see again in many of the better roodscreens.

In the church of St. Michael at Plea we shall find some paintings closely related to this splendid work, which is comparable in importance to the much earlier retable in Westminster Abbey.

Another feature which is peculiar to Norwich is one which was begun in the cloisters and extended all over the church ; that is, the carving of the bosses in the stone roof with subjects from the Bible and elsewhere (except in the choir, where the bosses only have heraldry and badges, and the Trinity and Assumption). The series is so interesting that a little more must be said about it, the cloisters being reserved for separate treatment.

The nave contains a great part of the Bible story, thus arranged :

I. In the first or easternmost bay is the Creation, Fall, and story of Cain and Abel.

II. Going westwards : The story of Noah and the Flood, the ark very conspicuous.

NORWICH CATHEDRAL: MISERICORDE—"SAMSON AND THE LION"

III. Tower of Babel, Abraham and the Angels, Abraham and Isaac, Jacob and Esau.

IV. Story of Jacob.

V. Story of Joseph—you may detect Joseph put into the pit, and sitting in the stocks.

VI. Story of Moses, the Finding, the Burning Bush, the Red Sea ; Samson and the Lion.

VII. Samson and the Gates, story of David and Goliath, Death of David, and Coronation of Solomon.

The Old Testament section ends here.

VIII. Life of Christ from the Annunciation to the Massacre of the Innocents.

IX. Flight into Egypt, Christ and the Doctors, Baptism, Temptation, Cana, Raising of Lazarus.

X. Entry into Jerusalem, Last Supper, Washing of Feet.

XI. The Agony, Betrayal, and Christ before Pilate.

XII. The Crucifixión, Entombment, Harrowing of Hell.

XIII. The Resurrection and Appearances, Ascension and Pentecost.

XIV. The Last Judgment, the Trinity, Bishop Lyhart, who built the roof : he was bishop from 1446 to 1473.

A very elaborate description of all these bosses was issued in a folio volume, in which they are all illustrated, by Dean Goulburn in 1876. In the above list I have only indicated the leading subjects of the eighteen which each bay contains.

The bosses of the transept roofs are very much later, and have never been fully described. They were made under Bishop Nykke (1501–36). Those in the north transept begin (perhaps) with the Birth of the Virgin, and carry on the story down to the Massacre of the Innocents. Those in the south begin with the Flight into Egypt, and give the history of part of the Ministry, including the Death of John Baptist, and some of the miracles of healing. There seems to be a good deal of repetition and dislocation in both series.

There is another set of storied bosses, in the Bauchun Chapel on the south side. This was made about 1460, and represents the story of the Chaste Empress, which is practically identical with Chaucer's Man of Lawe's Tale, and is to be seen very beautifully painted on the walls of Eton College Chapel.

Averting our eyes as much as possible from the west window of the cathedral (which is the gravest of insults to the memory of the excellent Bishop Stanley) we pass into the cloisters. These stand very high among the surviving cloisters of England. They took a long time to build. The earlier cloister was of wood, and perished in a great fire in 1272.

In 1297 the *east* walk was begun. In it is the beautiful entrance to the Chapter House, which was destroyed in the sixteenth century.

The *south* walk, south of which was the refectory, was the next to be built, and was begun early in the fourteenth century, to which period it all belongs.

The *west* walk came next, begun perhaps in 1377. In it are the lavatories for the monks to wash their hands at before they went into the refectory.

The *north* walk is of the early fifteenth century, and is said to have been finished in 1430. The Prior's door, the principal entrance into the church, is in the north-east corner ; a beautiful fourteenth-century work with figures carved round the arch (our Lord, angels, a bishop, a king, John Baptist, and Moses).

The *east* walk has fewer storied bosses than the others ; there are a few scenes from the Passion and the Evangelists.

In the *south* walk begins an elaborate series, illustrating the Revelation of St. John. This is continued all along the *west* walk ; only here some of the large bosses against the wall illustrate a couple of stories of Miracles of the Virgin.

The *north* walk has perhaps the most interesting and varied series of the four. It begins at the east end with the close of the Passion-story, from the Resurrection to Pentecost, and then has scenes from the lives of a number of well-known saints, e.g. the Virgin, SS. James, John, Clement, Giles, Thomas of Canterbury, Lucy, Martin, Katherine, George, Edmund, Denis, Eustace (a full description by me was published in 1911 by the Norfolk & Norwich Archæological Society).

This passion for storied bosses did not prevail to the same extent anywhere outside Norwich. One or two of the city churches (e.g. St. Stephen) have specimens. But they are neck-breaking things to study.

Of the monastic buildings the Chapter House, we have seen, is gone. The refectory is a roofless ruin, and there are remains of the infirmary.

Two fine gates lead into the close. The Erpingham gate is the better. We read of Sir Thomas Erpingham, the builder, in *Henry V.* The images on it, some of seated figures writing, some of apostles, and some of virgin saints, are of very good style ; small scrolls with the word *yenk* (= think : the thorn-letter is written as *y*) are of frequent occurrence. The upper part of the Ethelbert gate, with its flint-work, is modern. Just inside the Erpingham gate on the left is the ancient Grammar School, a fourteenth-century building which was founded as a chapel to St. John.

The second great historic building in Norwich is the castle. The ancient portion is confined to the immense keep, built by Roger Bigod in the twelfth century. This is surrounded by a congeries of nineteenth-century buildings : until 1887 the castle was the county gaol. The whole is now converted into a museum, and one of the very best provincial museums in the kingdom. The collection of birds can hardly be surpassed : here you may see the Last of the Bustards, shot at Lexham in 1838. The pictures of the Norwich school are deservedly famous, too, and the local antiquities uncommonly good. Some few manuscripts of considerable interest are exhibited : one of these is an early fourteenth-century Book of Hours, of very fine East Anglian work. In short, no one ought to leave the Castle Museum unvisited.

Another museum, of what may be called domestic antiquities, of very high interest is housed in an important fifteenth-century building known as *Strangers' Hall*, in St. Andrew's Street.

. The old *Guildhall* (1407–13) in the market-place is the last of the civic buildings which I shall notice. Its flint-work exterior is fine. In it there are remains of old glass. Blomefield has a good deal to say of the portions which existed in his time—the story of the corrupt judge who was flayed by Cambyses, and the legendary judgment of Solomon, who made three brothers—competitors for their father's estate—shoot at the corpse of their father, and awarded the estate to the youngest, who refused. There was also a picture of the Biblical Judgment of Solomon. How much will an intelligent visitor decipher ? I fear little is left. But the fittings of the court-room and the corporation plate are very notable.

Not civic in origin is *St. Andrew's Hall*, the nave of the Dominican church. Very few friars' churches are left in England, and this is a stately specimen. The nave is now the scene of the Norwich Musical Festivals and other gatherings, and has portraits of Norwich worthies. The tower which separated the nave from the choir is gone : it was a pretty hexagonal structure, and fell in 1712. The choir, still in being, but swept clean of ancient fittings, was the Dutch church. The conventual buildings were on the north, and there are considerable remains of them, particularly three sides of the cloister, vaulted, but with little ornament.

And now for the city churches. There are, or were, thirty-six old ones, but I can only suggest a small selection to be visited.

Foremost and largest, *St. Peter Mancroft*, in the market-place, very grand, with the best bells in Norwich in its fine tower. The nave arcades, within, are splendid. So is the remarkable Baldacchino over the font. The great east window is almost all of old glass, only the central light and two panels at the bottom of the adjacent lights are wholly new. The tracery lights are full of small figures of saints, many of them English, e.g. Alban, Kenelm, Oswald, Edward Martyr, and Edward Confessor, Edgar, Dubritius (?). The main lights contain parts of the early Life and the Passion of Christ, the Funeral of the Virgin, and a Life of St. Peter, besides several panels with donors. A careful chart of the window as now arranged is there for inspection : not quite correct perhaps in all points ; for instance, what is really a picture of St. Francis receiving the stigmata is, I think, wrongly described.

In the vestry, besides a couple of handsome manuscripts, there is a Nottingham alabaster panel representing virgin saints (Katherine, Ursula or Christina, Margaret, Helena, Barbara, one uncertain to me, and Etheldreda). Another panel of the same set is at *St. Stephen's*, to which we will go next. The porch has storied bosses of St. Stephen and Laurence. The east window is full of fine glass, partly *in situ*, partly foreign. The Rev. D. Harford has written a careful study of it (*Norf. Arch. Soc.*, vol. xv), from which I draw. The original glass is of 1533, and had a Crucifixion and two types thereof—the Sacrifice of Isaac and the Brazen Serpent (as in *St. Andrew's*). Relics of these three subjects may be discerned. Pieces of lettering also remain, which show that in some window in the church there was a Life of Stephen. In the tracery lights are small saints, as usual. The rest of the window is of foreign imported glass. The largest pieces represent : (on right) a St. John Baptist, from a Last Judgment ; an Apostle (centre) ; St. Christopher (left) ; and donors (right and left). These pieces, by the aid of heraldry and inscriptions, Mr. Harford has traced to a monastic church in the Eifel district, that of Mariawald, Heimbach. The alabaster panel preserved here represents a group of prophets (Isaiah with saw, etc.) headed by John Baptist. I imagine that both this and the other at St. Peter Mancroft belong to a Last Judgment.

St. Andrew's was rebuilt in 1506 : all that I wish to notice here is the glass in the north aisle, in three windows. One has only fragments and shields. The next has Abraham and Isaac, carrying a faggot, going up to Mount Moriah, and the Brazen Serpent. These were the side-pieces to a Crucifixion (as at St. Stephen's), and were once in the east window. The third has Death leading away a bishop, and the notes of an old Norwich antiquary, Kirkpatrick, show that there was a whole Dance of Death in the church. Ignorant of these notes, I have said in print that the subject was from the legend of St. Fridolin : I apologize and retract.

NORWICH : CHURCH OF ST. GREGORY—CLOSING RING

St. Peter Hungate had in Blomefield's time interesting glass commemorative of a rector, Thomas Andrew, who died in 1468, and a little of this is left in the east window. There is in fact a fair amount of fragmentary old glass in the church—Apostles, and Angels bearing the several clauses of the *Nunc Dimittis*, probably from Th. Andrew's window.

St. Michael at Plea.—The remarkable paintings on wood, to which

I have already alluded, have in part been made up into a reredos. Some must be from retables, some from a screen. The subjects are : the Betrayal, the Annunciation, St. Erasmus holding the windlass on which *horribile dictu* his entrails were wound out of him (but the story is fabulous), a Crucifixion, St. Thomas of Canterbury, St. Margaret, another Crucifixion, and (separate) the Resurrection.

St. Gregory's has a beautiful metal door-handle, a fine brass eagle of 1496, an ancient pall and cope, and a wall-painting of St. George and the Dragon.

St. Michael at Coslany is rather famous for the amount and the fine quality of its external flint-work, especially on a chapel added in Henry VII's time.

Add to these *St. Helen's*, converted in part to the uses of a " hospital ": a floor is run through it. There is a roof with storied bosses, e.g. of the Assumption of the Virgin ; there is also some good seating, and there is a pretty little cloister and refectory. Here you may purchase swans for your eating ; they are specially fed. The hospital to which the church is now attached is that of St. Giles, founded about 1230 by Bishop Suffield.

Let it not be supposed that Norwich does not offer many other buildings and prospects well worth looking at. I have only tried to pick out the salient ones.

In passing from Norwich to the county of Norfolk as a whole, I find myself animated by much the same emotions as either the Rev. J. Evans or Mr. John Britton, whichever was the author of the Norfolk volume in the *Beauties of England and Wales*, in the year 1809. " Though the topographer may shrink under the load of responsibility that oppresses his mind in contemplating the vastness and variety of the subjects which are necessarily embraced, yet his curiosity and zeal will be constantly kept alert, and he will be induced to prosecute his task with some degree of cheerfulness, under the conviction that the liberal reader will appreciate his works with lenity, and scrutinize them with candour."

Again I say, an obstacle has been the question where to begin. It seems easiest on the whole to take the—

SOUTH-EAST QUARTER

first, since it is neatly marked off by the roads and railways eastward to Yarmouth and southward to Tivetshall. Places which lie conveniently near these routes either on west or north will be included.

First going nearly due south we come to *Arminghall*, which had a fine old manor-house of the Mingays, whose porch of the fourteenth century was said to have come from the Carmelites of Norwich. Is it still there? I could not find it.

Then *Caistor St. Edmund*, perhaps the most important Roman site in the county, at which excavations have recently been going on, and have resulted in the discovery of the foundations of twin small temples, as well as other public and private buildings. The area is well marked out; extensive remains of the walls render it much more impressive than many of the Roman places in this country. A contribution to the excavation fund will be money well spent.

It will be of no use to rely upon Keyser's (most useful) manual of *Buildings having Mural Decorations* (South Kensington Museum, 1883) and go to *Poringland*, in hope of finding the screen he describes : it is gone, together with a great deal else that Blomefield saw there. There is some good seating. The building is one of the odd-looking ones which have a clerestory and no aisle. Fine old houses are near the church.

We are now fairly on the Norwich–Bungay road, and we pass *Brooke*, which used to have interesting wall-paintings of the Seven Deadly Sins, and (somewhat to the east) *Seething*, where more paintings —the Three Dead, etc., and St. Christopher among them—were uncovered only a year or two ago, but have since (by no means to the credit of Seething wisdom) been re-covered with what is described as temporary whitewash. The Seven Sacraments font has been so recut as to be without interest.

A little farther south, and we pass the handsome brick Hall of *Hedenham*, and then we may turn west to *Denton* and *Alburgh*. *Denton* Church stands prettily, and has a number of interesting features : a north porch with good carving (e.g. bosses of the Nativity and Ascension); a chest said to have been made up with painted panels from the screen, but the panels in question are unusually small. The twelve figures are : *east* end of chest, Agnes and Dorothy ; *south*, Jude, Peter, a bishop,

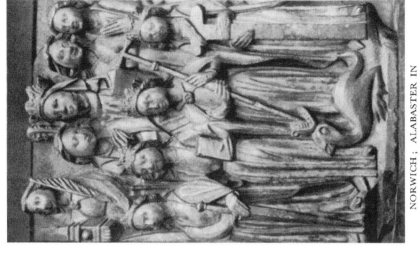

NORWICH; ALABASTER IN
ST. PETER MANCROFT CHURCH.

ATTLEBOROUGH CHURCH SCREEN.

one uncertain, Zita or Citha with rosary, Barbara, Edmund, Edward the Confessor ; *west*, Walstan in ermine with scythe, and Paul. Thirdly, there is the east window, put up by Mr. Postlethwayte in 1717, which is filled with glass, chiefly heraldic (of which a chart is in the church, and of which Mr. Clement Ingleby has written a careful account in his *Supplement to Blomefield*) ; there are also some large late foreign heads and some old roundels, one of St. Christopher. The piscina is remarkable, but how much of it is original ?

DENTON: BOSS IN NORTH PORCH

At *Alburgh* the reredos has the lower panels of the screen, on which are no figures, but pretty gesso work. There was a Christopher here in Blomefield's time ; and there are two bells of 1436.

We continue southward and come to *Starston*, where I fear there is little to be seen of a very fine wall-painting of about 1300 in a tomb recess, representing a soul being received into heaven. *Harleston* is a market town ; its mother church is *Redenhall*, which is an imposing building with a fine tower and famous peal of bells. Inside there is a fine brass eagle lectern and a wooden one as well, a screen with the twelve Apostles, and a chapel with monuments of the ancient family of Gawdy with heraldic glass, moved from Gawdy Hall, a moated house hard by.

Turning east we can follow the Waveney to *Earsham*, whose church has a good roof, and some quite interesting imported foreign glass, which has been recently well illustrated and described in Mr. Ingleby's *Supplement to Blomefield*. One very pretty panel is of Joseph and his brethren. Others are roundels with Bible pictures and heraldry. Near-by are *Geldeston*, scene of a once popular thriller, *The House in the Marsh*, and *Gillingham*, where the surviving church (there were two in the one churchyard) is good Norman, with apsidal end. At *Ditchingham* is a good specimen of the Three Dead and Three Living, in wall-painting. Then we may turn north-east and find *Aldeby*, site of a small priory whose picturesque buttressed buildings adjoin the churchyard; *Burgh St. Peter*, with a strange tower of five stages diminishing towards the top. It had also wall-paintings— Martyrdom of St. Thomas of Canterbury, Christopher, and Death of the Virgin — (how much is left I know not) ; *Haddiscoe*, where there is fine Norman work. The tower, and a sculptured figure over the south door, are particularly notable. There is also a St. Christopher.

With that we turn west to the Beccles–Norwich route and stop at *Loddon*. Here the church was built in the last years of the fifteenth century by Chief Justice Hobart (*d.* 1525). A late picture of him and his lady and the church is to be seen within. The building is a fine one of its date. The font has the Seven Sacraments, the eighth panel being our Lord in Majesty. The screen paintings are quite unusual, for they show for the most part scenes and not single figures. Reckoning from left to right we have, after two perished panels, half of one which may represent St. Anne. Then the Martyrdom of St. William of Norwich : he is bound saltire-wise to stakes, and Jews are wounding his side and receiving the blood in a basin. Then follow the Annunciation, Nativity, Circumcision, Adoration of the Magi, half of the Presentation, three blank panels, one with a figure holding up a dagger by the point, two more blank, and the Ascension. There is a good eighteenth-century recumbent effigy of a lady.

At *Chedgrave* there is some Norman work and some old Flemish glass in the east window. At *Langley* the north door is good Early English, and within there is more foreign glass. The east window has late panels with part of the Nativity and Adoration and French inscriptions (mixed up with modern glass). St. George and the Dragon is also old. In the nave windows are late foreign roundels with no rare subjects. *Langley Abbey* is passed on the road to Buckenham Ferry. It was a Premonstratensian house founded in 1198. The site is a farm, and there are considerable remains of the domestic buildings in and about the farmyard, mostly of course flint. A plan will be found in *Archæologia*, vol. 75.

Another route, again due south from Norwich, takes in *Mulbarton*, where is some glass ; the Expulsion from Paradise, Adam digging (the other half of this, Eve spinning, is at Martham), one of an Order of Angels, *Potestates*, of which others are also at Martham ; a St. Anne teaching the Virgin to read ; her book, inscribed *Domine labia*, etc. ; and some other figures. Next I mention *Tacolneston*. A few panels of a very remarkable screen are here. The shafts have beautiful gesso work, and there are borders painted on a white ground. Two painted scenes survive, of small size and very delicate work, which seem Flemish. They resemble miniatures in manuscripts ; both unhappily are much injured. One is of the Annunciation ; a window on left—a bed with red tester, and a picture hanging on the wall—the Virgin kneels at the foot of the bed, Gabriel in a cope is on the right. The other is the Temptation of St. Anthony. He is seated in front of his cell on a rocky landscape, and a richly dressed lady (but with fire about her feet !) holds up a covered gold vessel.

East of the railway are two places : *Fritton* the first, at which are wall-paintings of SS. Christopher and George, and a screen which, besides some Apostles and the four doctors of the Church, has pictures of Sir John Bacon and his family (*cir.* 1510) ; *Shelton* the other, a church quite out of the common. It is of fine brick, the clerestory faced with stone. Inside there is rich stone panelling, and niches between the arches of the arcades, and ten image-brackets on each side. The building is due to Sir Ralph Shelton (*d.* 1497), and his rebus of shell and tun is in glass in some of the window heads. In the east windows of chancel and aisles there is handsome glass. North aisle : Annunciation, Resurrection, a female saint with a male head,

9

Virgin and Child, shields of Wesynham and another.   South aisle :
late kneeling figures of man and lady ; shields of Bedyngsfeld, Schelton,

SHELTON: DETAIL OF TOMB OF SIR ROBERT HOUGHTON

and another.   Chancel—late and restored : six large shields and six
figures of donors, angel-musicians above.   The tomb of Sir Robert
Houghton is a fine one ; he is in judge's robes, and his two wives and

SCOLE: WHITE HART INN

131

son are with him. The font is of a type common in our counties, having lions on four faces, alternating with angels holding shields.

Proceeding down to *Diss* we join a road running along the Suffolk border. A little to the east is *Scole*, famous for a coaching inn (17th cent.)—still to be seen—and for its tremendous inn-sign, which formed a sort of triumphal arch across the road. I cannot help dwelling on this a little. It was paid for (to the tune of over £1,000) by one John Peck in 1655 ; the artist was Fairchild. In the composition which surmounted it were arms of Mr. Peck and the Norfolk nobility, supported by angels and lions, and also such impressive figures as Jonah and the whale, Charon, Cerberus, Actaeon, the Cardinal Virtues, and to crown all an astronomer seated on something which " by a secret device acted as an hygrometer " and faced to the rainy quarter. It was greatly thought of, and engravings of it may be seen ; but it has been cleared away. And west of Diss is *South Lopham*, whose fine Norman tower looks very imposing as seen from the road. We might continue to Thetford, but I believe it will be best to keep that for the next excursion and start from Norwich, as before. We will, however, pick up a few places that lie within range of Diss.

Winfarthing need not perhaps be visited unless for the ruins of its Great Oak ; but it finds mention because it had a relic (left by a thief, people said later, but I doubt this) called the Good Sword of Winfarthing, which had, I think, no exact parallel in this country. It helped to find lost property, especially horses ; and it " helped to the shortening of a married man's life, if that the wife who was weary of her husband would set a candle before that sword every Sunday for the space of a whole year, no Sunday excepted, for then all was vain whatsoever was done before." St. Uncumber did something like this, but on the whole it reminds one more of Wales and Brittany than England (and St. Uncumber was foreign also). Then there is *Kenninghall* with a good Norman doorway bearing a horse and a lion, and notable benches and font-cover. Also the Royal arms of Elizabeth. At *Banham* note the base of the tower, and a wooden effigy of a knight of the fourteenth century, painted stone-colour.

The *Buckenhams, Old* and *New.*—The church tower of the latter has exceptionally fine work round its base, continued along the aisle walls ; the roof-brackets inside are heads of apostles and prophets. At *Old Buckenham* are remains of a castle of William d'Albini, and there was a Priory of Austin Canons. Its shield is in a window in the church, which has a polygonal tower.

SOUTH-WEST QUARTER

Again we start from Norwich, and take the Wymondham-Attleborough direction. There is not a great deal on the eastern side of the road before we get to Wymondham, but *Eaton*, adjacent to

KENNINGHALL: ROYAL ARMS

Norwich, has good wall-paintings, including a Martyrdom of St. Thomas of Canterbury, and several single figures of saints. We may divert to *Ketteringham*, which has fine monuments of Heveninghams, and *Ashwellthorpe*, where an alabaster tomb of Sir Edmund de Thorpe and his lady is perhaps even better. There is also a sixteenth-century chest with a representation of a siege upon it.

Wymondham, however, is really remarkable. The priory church at

WYMONDHAM CHURCH, FROM THE EAST

134

once causes surprise, because it has a tower at each end. How is this ? The priory was founded in 1107 by William d'Albini as a cell to the Abbey of St. Albans, and in the course of the twelfth century a very large Norman church was built. It consisted of a nave of twelve bays up to the central tower, transepts with an apsidal chapel on the east side of each, a choir of three bays, and an apse, with aisles which also had apses. There were two towers at the west end. Of this there now remain nine bays of the nave with aisles—the south aisle is of post-Reformation date. At the east end of the nave is a screen wall, which supports the west side of an octagonal tower built at the very end of the fourteenth century, and replacing the original central tower which stood farther east.

The clerestory and the nave roof and the north aisle are additions of the middle of the fifteenth century. At that time also the two western towers were pulled down and the present splendid stately west tower of flint erected. This was the work of the townspeople, who were always at odds with the monks, the latter from time to time claiming rights over the whole church, which they failed to establish.

After the Dissolution in 1538 the whole of the eastern part of the church was pulled down, leaving only scanty traces. The Norman plan of this part had also been changed : the central and northern apses had been turned into square-ended structures, and the choir appreciably lengthened. This reconstruction was done it seems at the time when the present octagonal tower was built. It was a very common practice to substitute square ends for apses in churches large and small throughout the country.

The nave has survived, of course, because it was the parish church. It is a splendid fragment, comparable to Norwich and Ely. The fifteenth-century hammer-beam roof is a fine example. On the south side of the altar an arch is filled up with a terra-cotta erection of the early sixteenth century, very unusual and beautiful with its delicate Renaissance detail. It is in the form of sedilia, and it is described as the monument of the last *Abbot*, Ferrers (for after being for most of its life a priory dependent on St. Albans, the house was made into an independent abbey in 1448). Of other furniture there is a good font, an organ case of about 1790, and some little enamel glass in the north aisle, besides a chandelier and lectern. The recent work in the choir is well worth examination.

WYMONDHAM: "THE GREEN DRAGON"

Outside, the remains of the monastic buildings are few and shapeless; you can trace the position of the cloister on the south. In the usual place, leading out of the cloister on the east, was the Chapter House, of which the eastern gable is the largest bit of ruin that survives. This building was originally apsidal and altered to a square end. A well of St. Thomas à Becket is near the church, and a chapel of his now serves as the Grammar School. It is worth a visit, an aisleless building with a fine arch just inside the west end. There were side chapels, or a side chapel on the south. The Market Cross (1616) will not be unremarked; nor the " Green Dragon " Inn.

Attleborough.—Here legend says that St. Edmund resided for a year, and learnt the Psalter ; and the book from which he learnt was said to have existed at Bury Abbey down to a later date. But I do not know that legend is to be trusted. What Attleborough has now to show is a very fine church, of which the choir, now destroyed, was the church of a College of Holy Cross, a late fourteenth-century foundation of Sir Robert Mortimer. The tower, formerly central, is now at the east end ; it is of Norman work. The transepts are rather short, and being at the east end are more or less cut off from use. The organ is in one of them.

The remarkable feature in the furnishing is the screen, now placed at the west end ; it was formerly just west of the tower, and had altars before it. It retains its upper stage with late paintings of the arms of the old English sees upon it. In the stage below are six close panels, forming two retables, with rather obliterated paintings. On one side are John Baptist, the Virgin and Child, John Evangelist. On the other are smaller figures : an Archbishop, the Trinity (" Italian," i.e. the Father supporting the Crucified Son), St. Bartholomew. These have below them inscriptions commemorative of donors. English texts from the Bible of Elizabethan date have been added, and there is on the lower stage a somewhat older painting of the Cross, with crown of thorns and title and Latin inscription. In its original position this screen was surmounted by a great wall-painting above the tower arch, which disappeared in 1848. It represented a large rood with prophets, angels, and other accessories. The fourteenth-century west window has exceptionally fine tracery.

Now let me give (for once) an example of past glories which might easily have survived. Of *Snetterton* Blomefield says that " over the rood was a defaced painting of the Last Day ; on the top our Saviour on the Judgment-seat. *Come, ye blessed,* etc. *Depart, ye cursed,* etc. The windows contain the history of the *Revelation,* with the Apostles, each bearing a sentence of the Creed in a label from his mouth.' The east window of the north aisle was filled with angels supporting arms (which are specified). Other windows in this aisle had the history of the Creation, of Christ's baptism, of St. Christopher, etc., with the legends in labels, and there were other remains of glass commemorating Robert Spylman, rector about 1450, when all this glazing was put in. And where — one is tempted to ask — where the Blue Blazes has it all gone to since 1730? for there is nothing of it to be found at Snetterton now.

HARLING : HERALDIC SCREEN-PANEL

We do, however, find something quite appreciable at *East Harling.* The handsome church (with a spire, not very common in Norfolk, and a pretty parapet) has several claims on our attention. Fifteenth-century tombs of Sir Robert Harling (1435) and Sir Thomas Lovell. A screen which has *carved* quatrefoils, most of them heraldic, but one with a rood and Mary and John, the cross being a tree growing out of the loins of the reclining Jesse. Glass : the whole east window is full of fifteenth-century glass given by a Sir Robert Wingfield (*d.* 1480), and long preserved at the Hall, but put back in the eighteenth century. The subjects, from the early life and the Passion of Christ, are easily legible. There are also St. Mary Magdalene, a bishop-saint, Sir Robert and bits of his wife ; and inscribed scrolls in the lower part of the window show fragments of the *Te Deum* : " Tu d(evicto mortis aculeo) Tu ad dexteram (dei sedes) (Judex) crederis esse venturus," etc. There are pieces of glass in other windows too : in the north aisle, angels and a young king.

After this we are out on the heath, and I note nothing before *Thetford*. Thetford, we have seen, was a bishop's see (from 1070 to 1091 only), but that is not by any means its only attraction. Few towns of its size are fuller of old remains. First is a secular one, the Castle hill, which stands in a very prettily planted park-like area, and is one of the most impressive earth-works I have seen. The central mound is a magnificent erection. Tradition connects it with the battles fought with the Danes about the time of St. Edmund's martyrdom ; but I suppose it is really of Norman date. Then the Cluniac priory, of which the large fifteenth-century gatehouse is seen from the station. The remains of the domestic buildings are in private grounds, but the ruins of the church are accessible ; the plan has been investigated in recent years (see Dr. Fairweather's account and plan *apud* Ingleby's *Supplement*).

Founded by Roger Bigod in 1104, the church was probably planned about 1107. It had a nave of eight bays, two western towers, short transepts with an apsidal chapel apiece, and an aisled choir originally apsidal but extended in the thirteenth century, when a large chapel of the Virgin was built on the north to contain an ancient image of the Virgin that came to light there after a period of neglect. It was found to have a large number of relics concealed in it, and became an object of pilgrimage.

There is little of the stone facing and detail left in these ruins, which are chiefly masses of flint ; but some there is of good quality. The cloisters were on the south of the church, and the refectory is or was traceable.

The next most considerable ruin is that of a Benedictine nunnery just outside the town on the Suffolk side. The buildings of this survived almost untouched, I believe, down to the eighteenth century—I judge from Thomas Martin's description in his *History of Thetford*. The church has in recent years been turned into a racing stable (!), and I do not know how far it is accessible ; but there are considerable remains of the Norman crossing (i.e. piers of the central tower and transept).

In the precincts of the Grammar School is a flint ruin locally called the cathedral ; if it was the cathedral, it was later on a Dominican friary. On the Brandon road are the more picturesque remains of the house of the Canons of the Holy Sepulchre (see the Introduction), and in the grounds of Ford Place are those of a house of Austin Friars founded by John of Gaunt in 1387.

The King's House is a good one, and in it are preserved the collections of Prince Frederick Duleep Singh, which he bequeathed to the town. The " Bell Inn " is also notable. The three churches that remain out of a traditional twenty are none of them specially interesting.

If we progress farther west we come to *Weeting*, famous for the primeval flint mines called *Grimes' Graves*—accessible by permit from the estate office. *Bromehill* Priory (Augustinian) was in this parish, and some remains of it are to be seen. The churches of *Feltwell* and *Hockwold*, farther west, have each of them some features worth seeing ; but more so *Northwold*, for there is one of the best Easter sepulchres, with the watching soldiers sculptured on the front of the tomb, and fine tabernacle work above. Here we are on the edge of the fen. Turning back to Thetford, we find near it on the east *Rushford* (or *Rushworth*), where Edmund Gonville, founder of Gonville Hall in Cambridge, established in 1326 a college of priests, of which two sides of the court, now the rectory, remain. There was a similar foundation at *Thompson* (near Stow Bedon), now a farmhouse. *Rushford* College certainly deserves a visit.

If now we return from Thetford to Norwich, taking a some-what north-easterly direction, we shall pass within range of *Breckles*, with a noted sixteenth-century house ; *Griston* (screen and a little glass) ; *Watton* (undistinguished except that near it the death of the Babes in the Wood is located, in Wayland or Wailing

Wood) ; *Carbrooke*, where the church stands high and well, and has good screen and roof and some armour ; *Scoulton*, with a famous mere ; and then we come to *Hingham*. The church of Hingham is a very stately building, of the fourteenth century in the main. The flint tower (15th cent.) is one of the most splendid in Norfolk. Inside, besides the beauty of the arcade, two things call for description : first, the glass in the east window, which was given by one of the Kimberley family, and is fine German work of the sixteenth century. There are four large pictures each filling three lights, and in the central light two saints. The pictures are : (1) upper left—the Crucifixion, with the thieves—angel and devil -taking their souls ; (2) upper right—Christ in glory ; surrounded by groups of apostles and of Old Testament saints, Adam, Eve, Moses, David, Melchizedek ; (3) lower left—the Deposition and Entombment (small) ; (4) lower right—the Harrowing of Hell and Resurrection : the latter sur-rounded by the appearances of Christ to the women, to Thomas, and to Peter. The two saints are perhaps Thomas, and certainly Anne carrying the Virgin and Child. Second, the great tomb on the north side of the chancel to Thomas Lord Morley (*d.* 1435). It may be of interest to note the images of saints which remain in the recessing of the main arch : they are (on the right from the bottom)—George, a bishop, Michael, a seraph ; at top—Christ. On left, descending—Mary Magdalene, Margaret, John Evangelist (?), Katherine. In the side turrets are small images of angels. At the summit is the Judge, with kneeling donors (?), and below, Gabriel and the Virgin : ten kneeling figures are at the back and sides of the tomb, which is a very exceptional structure, the work (say Pryor and Gardner) of the same craftsmen as the Erpingham gate at Norwich.

North-east is *Barnham Broom*, where the screen has the following interesting series of figures (reckoning from the left) : after three blank panels SS. Clement with his anchor, Walstan with his two oxen, a defaced bishop, an aged king, perhaps Edward the Confessor, Etheldreda as a crowned abbess, Edmund with three arrows, With-burga, a deer leaping up to her, Dorothy, and Elizabeth of Thuringia with cup and loaves.

Somewhat south-east, *Wramplingham* has a fine Early English chancel with six splayed lancet windows on each side ; in the heads are some fourteenth-century canopies in old glass, but no figures : Blomefield records a series of apostles in these windows.

I have told the story of St. Walstan of *Bawburgh* above. In the church here is no picture of him, but there is a certain amount of old glass—St. Katherine, St. Barbara, part of an Annunciation, several angels, and roundels made up of fragments.

So we pass into Norwich by *Earlham*, which figures in Borrow's *Lavengro* (though unnamed), in Hare's *Gurneys of Earlham*, and most pleasantly and memorably in Percy Lubbock's *Earlham*.

MID-EAST NORFOLK

The next route shall be eastward, including Yarmouth. On the way thither we will first take the Burlinghams. *South Burlingham* has some wall-paintings, part of a Christopher, an earlier fragment of St. George and the Dragon next to it and overlapped by it ; and on the south wall of the chancel, a fourteenth-century Martyrdom of St. Thomas of Canterbury. The church is on the left, the four knights on the right. There is also a good fifteenth-century pulpit with painting, inscribed with the text : "Inter natos mulierum non surrexit maior Johanne Baptista." Some of the benches have pretty openwork carving.

North Burlingham has two churches. St. Andrew, the larger of the two (St. Peter's is but a fragment without a tower), has an excellent screen. The saints have their names, and reading from the left are as follows : *S. Withburga*, crowned, holding a church—two deer leap up to her ; *S. Benedictus Abbas*, two devils at his feet ; *S. Edwardus Rex*, the Confessor, with a ring ; *S. Thomas* (of Canterbury), defaced—an inscribed date appears to be 1530 ; *S. Johannes Baptista*, with lamb ; *S. Cecilia*, with wreath and palm ; *S. Walstanus*, crowned, barefoot, with scythe, wearing ermined cope, and purse at girdle ; *S. Katherina virgo*, with sword and wheel ; a defaced man ; a fragment of *S. Etheldreda* as abbess. Two panels at the beginning of the series are blank. The roof has painted angels.

At *Acle* we may first take the road to the south, and see (if we desire wall-paintings) *Moulton*, which has a headless Christopher on the north wall, and on the south the Works of Mercy under a painted arcade. The deeds of charity are being done by a woman, and there are traces of a figure of Christ, but the sick, the prisoner, and the burial of the dead have disappeared. The Early English piscina is good, and the place is remote and pretty. Then *Wickhampton*, where the paintings are more visible in drawings published in Ingleby's *Supplement* than on the walls. Still they are important. They consist of a Christopher, a very elaborate Three Dead and Three Living (late 14th cent.), with a huntsman and hare, and the Works of Mercy in two rows, one of which is headed by a figure of the risen Christ. Here again the works are done by a woman, and there have been scrolls in English, none of which is fully legible : the prison scene with a man in the stocks, and the burial with the sexton casting earth on the corpse and the priest sprinkling it, are the most noteworthy.

The vast dead flats inland from Yarmouth are very impressive. One remembers David Copperfield on the coach that had to fight its way seaward in the great storm, which is perhaps Dickens's finest piece of description. The tower of *Halvergate* dominates this region.

Our road from Acle will take us round the edge of the flat, going north and east, and here we are in a region of names ending in the Danish *-by*. The first I take note of is *Filby*. Here the screen shows a good quality of painting. The saints represented are (from left) Cecilia with a wreath of roses, a fine St. George in white mantle and gold armour, Katherine, Peter in gold robe, Paul, Margaret carrying an elaborate cross and rising out of the dragon, Michael with scales in ermined cape, and Barbara with palm and tower.

Caister-by-Yarmouth comes next. It was, of course, a Roman station, but the remains of the camp are negligible. The attraction is the castle, an early specimen of brick, built by Sir John Fastolf about 1443. Sir John is quite undeservedly branded as a coward in the French wars (see 1 *Henry VI*), and has besides got mixed up in our minds with Falstaff ; indeed, after Shakespeare had under pressure substituted the name of Falstaff for his original Oldcastle, there were still complaints that he was defaming the memory of Fastolf. Fastolf (who was forceful but hardly amiable) died in 1459, and the castle went to the Pastons, was claimed by Thomas Mowbray Duke of Norfolk, and taken after a long siege. Then it came back to the Pastons, and was theirs till the middle of the seventeenth century. William of Worcester, a secretary of Fastolf, tells of a second siege and capture by Lord Scales.

It is a picturesque ruin, moated, with one large tower at the north-west ; formerly it surrounded a quadrangle, the great hall being on the west side. The south and east sides are gone. To the east are the remains of a church.

Then *Yarmouth*. The visitor who comes to enjoy himself here needs no guiding from me, and when he wants to see the curiosities of the place, they are fairly obvious. The immense church of St. Nicholas is the first : a cruciform building with aisles—very broad (112 ft.), often restored and not containing many noteworthy ancient fittings, but exceedingly imposing. The organ case, which has been divided and placed on the floor, is a magnificent specimen ; both fronts of it are well worth examination. There is some glass in the northern windows, apparently German of the early sixteenth century and of good quality : a bust of St. Andrew, two red-winged angels, and other pieces.

The Fisherman's Hospital (1702) is hard by. The cupola, with a statue of St. Peter which crowns the front side of the quadrangle, is very successful, and the whole building picturesque. The Tol-house, containing the town museum, is partly of the fourteenth century. Behind it are some interesting remains of the Dominican friary. When you have seen the dungeon below the Tolhouse you should read about Sarah Martin, " the prisoners' friend," and realize that there can have been few better people.

Leaving Yarmouth by the Caister road again and going north we can deal with the whole—

NORTH-EAST QUARTER

of the county. This region includes what is known as Broadland (though there are Broads south of this, between Yarmouth and Lowestoft). Broadland abounds in holiday attractions, of which it is not my function to tell. But I think it necessary to warn the dry-land explorer that he will find his way made very tortuous by the existence of the Broads, and will do well to keep a careful eye on the map.

Our area shall be bounded on the west by the road from Cromer by Aylsham to Norwich, and we are starting from the south-east corner of it.

Martham is our first stop. Here the church has fine doors, a Seven Sacraments font with Christ as Judge in the eighth panel, and two windows (the eastern ones of the aisles) filled with fifteenth-century glass. The north aisle has in the tracery a human-headed serpent

LUDHAM: DETAIL OF THE SCREEN, WITH ST. AUGUSTINE
AND ST. AMBROSE

from a picture of the Fall, scenes from the Life of Christ, viz. the Crowning with Thorns, Resurrection, and Ascension ; single figures of saints, Juliana with a devil in a chain, Edmund, Agnes, Margaret.

10

The south has several figures from a set of the Nine Orders of Angels, several apostles, Eve spinning—part of a subject from Mulbarton (where also are more of the Orders of Angels). The chancel is rather terrible florid modern work.

At *West Somerton*, remote and quiet, are wall-paintings, rather faint, of the early fourteenth century. A large Last Judgment on the south wall of the nave (not the usual place), and a Christopher. On the north wall has been a series of the Passion. The Entry into Jerusalem, the Scourging, and the Resurrection, are or have been decipherable. These read from the west.

At *Potter Heigham* is a good deal of painting on walls and screen. North wall : Christopher, headless ; eastward : an appearance of large leaves and a large nimbed figure holding a round object ; also the Works of Mercy (in two rows)—a woman is the heroine. A very obscure painting adjoins it which I thought might illustrate the story of St. Katherine. On the south wall a nice female head in outline, and over the chancel arch the remains of a Doom. The screen has the Evangelists and the Four Doctors and Seynt Loye alias Eligius, with his blacksmith's hammer.

Ludham has a very uncommon feature, namely, the painting of the Crucifixion, which surmounts the screen. The boards on which it is were found in the rood-loft staircase. They now fill the head of the chancel arch. It is not easy to read the figures apart from those of the Christ, the Virgin, and John, but two seraphs seem to be at the sides, and there are two other personages who have been thought to be Longinus the centurion and Mary Magdalene. On the other face of the boards (which were turned round for the purpose) are a Protestant substitute in the shape of the Royal Arms of Elizabeth, and a text. Ludham screen is also a good example ; an inscription carved on the sills of the arches says : Pray for the sowle of John . . . and Cycyly his wyf that gave forten pounde and for alle other benefactors. made in the year of ower lord god MCCCCLXXXXIII°. The saints have their names inscribed : from the left they are—Mary Magdalene, Stephen, Edmund, Henricus Sextus, Augustine, Ambrose, Gregory, Jerome, Edward Confessor, Walstan as king with scythe, Laurence, Apollonia with tooth in forceps. From this place you can reach *St. Benet's Hulme* by a walk, but it is most easily approachable by water. This is really the oldest

ST. BENET'S HULME: THE GATEHOUSE

abbey in Norfolk, but there is very little left of it. The gatehouse is the most conspicuous of the remains. Here is an annoying circumstance : Henry VIII made the bishop of Norwich exchange the estates of Hulme for those of Norwich (much more valuable, of course), and until quite recent times the bishop, when his turn came to be summoned to the House of Lords, was summoned as Abbot of Hulme— thus being the only surviving mitred abbot. Then red tape said, Why should this anomaly be allowed to subsist ?, made the writ conform to all the rest, and wiped out a nice little harmless piece of history.

Ranworth may as well be taken next, lying as it does fairly near Hulme (though hardly accessible thence by road). Ranworth screen is the most famous of all, I think, in the country. It differs from others in having two projecting wings, separating off two so-called retables on north and south.

The paintings are not surpassed by any in quality. The medium is partly oil ; the diapering and ornamentation generally both rich and delicate. Mr. Aymer Vallance traces Spanish influence in them. The figures on the north retable, which like those on the south have angels above them, are St. Etheldreda, St. John Baptist : or is it St. Agnes, with a lamb on a book ? ; St. John Baptist certainly ; St. Barbara. On the projecting wing (south face) : a splendid St. George and two smaller figures, a bishop who may be St. Felix, and St. Stephen.

On the central portion of the screen the Apostles in this order : Simon with fish, Thomas, Bartholomew, James the Great, Andrew, Peter, Paul, John, Philip (basket of loaves), James the Less, Jude (boat), Matthew. South wing (northern face) : two smaller figures, St. Lawrence, and an archbishop (St. Thomas of Canterbury ?) ; larger figure, St. Michael with feathered body—very fine.

Southern retable : St. Mary, mother of James, with her children James and John ; the Virgin and Child ; St. Mary of Cleophas with two children, one (Jude) holding a boat ; St. Margaret.

There is also a remarkable painted wooden lectern with an eagle of St. John, and *Gloria tibi domine*, etc., with four lines of music.

Reverting to Ludham we will go north to *Catfield*. Here were many wall-paintings above the arches. Very little is left on the north, but a figure lying in bed, which might belong to the Seven Sacraments (recorded here). On the south is a man poking a fire—the burning, I thought, of the philosophers whom St. Katherine converted—or

STALHAM: FONT PANEL—"THE BAPTISM OF CHRIST"

else St. John in the cauldron of oil. There was a Wheel of Fortune, a Tree of the Deadly Sins, the Virtues (? Works of Mercy) on the north, and a number of New Testament scenes, besides St. Katherine and St. Lawrence on the south. It would be well worth while to try to retrieve these.

The screen has sixteen figures, all of kings ; I can only be certain of the sixth from north, St. Olaf with a battle-axe, and the first on

BARTON TURF : SCREEN-PANEL—
HENRY VI

south, St. Edmund.

Irstead may come in for a word here. It has wall-paintings of angels and an apostle-screen ; but I have not seen it.

Going northward again we come to *Stalham*. The font here has figures of the Apostles and of the Trinity and the Baptism of Christ on the bowl, and of sainted kings round the base, with the Virgin and Child ; here again we can see St. Olaf and St. Edmund. Another has a covered cup, and another a staff stuck through a wreath. The screen panels h a v e b e e n scrubbed : they have Edmund, another king, Andrew, Rochus the plague saint showing his sore (he is a late foreign im- portation), and Thomas of Canterbury.

If we make a diversion west and south we shall get to *Small- burgh*, where the screen was in part painted over (I have not seen it) and *Tunstead*, where is a good example with the Apostles and Four Doctors, and also the

rood beam, and a curious stone platform behind the altar for the exhibition of relics, perhaps.

More important is *Barton Turf*, with the second best screen in the county. There are two portions, one of late fourteenth century, the other of fifteenth. On the first and larger from left are : St. Apollonia, St. Citha or Zita with purse, keys, and rosary, and then a fine set of the Nine Orders :

Potestates, armed, with a devil in a chain, and scourge.
Vertutes, four-winged, with cap, sceptre, feathered body and legs.
Dominaciones, four-winged, in triple crown, and chasuble.
Seriphyn, six-winged, feathered body, girdle of fire, censer.
Cherubin, six wings, full of eyes, feathered body, linen girdle, hands outspread.

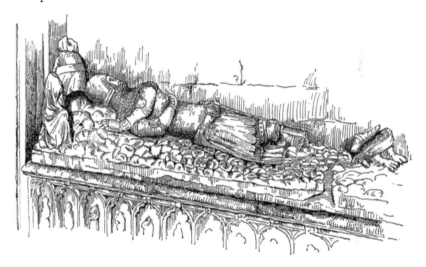

INGHAM : EFFIGY OF SIR OLIVER DE INGHAM

Principatus, four-winged, girdle with bells ; holds a glass vial and a palm.
Troni, six-winged, long-sleeved robe ; holds a church and a pair of scales.
Archangeli, two-winged, in plate armour ; stands in a citadel, and holds mace and sword.
Angeli, in alb, an alms-box at the girdle ; holds a spear. Two naked souls on a rock, praying.
(*Thrones* ought properly to follow *Cherubin*.)
The last figure is St. Barbara.

On the later section of the screen are :
Henry VI, without a nimbus, Edmund, Edward Confessor, and
Holofius, i.e. Olaf with a battle-axe and two loaves (punning on his
name).

Picking up the road again at Stalham we have *Ingham* Church, a
very fine building. The rather shapeless remains of a priory founded
by Sir Miles Stapleton are attached to it on the north side. Within
there is an exceptionally fine tomb (north of chancel) of Sir Oliver de
Ingham (14th cent.), who lies, as if ready to spring up in a moment,
with his arms oddly crossed. There was painting at the back of
the arch once, but it is invisible. Another excellent tomb is that of
Sir Roger de Bois and his lady. There are four admirable statuettes,
and at the east end a Trinity between angels who bear up souls.
The brasses here must, judging by their indents, have been splendid.
Rubbings of them do exist in the British Museum.

Hempstead and *Lessingham*, north of Ingham, are two churches with
screen-paintings, and rather curious ones. At Hempstead the figures
include John of Bridlington, a fourteenth-century canon of that house,
who somehow gained the reputation of a prophet, and more deservedly
that of a holy man ; for the prophecies in Latin verse attributed to
him are pretty certainly none of his making. There is also St. Theobald, whether the one of Provins (11th cent.) or the Abbot of Vaux de
Cernay (13th cent.) I am not clear : each of them was a courtly knight
in early life, and the picture is of a man with hawk on hand. We
have also Erasmus, Blaise, Francis, Giles, and Juliana. *Lessingham*
has the Apostles, and the Doctors and St. Giles have been painted
on paper (16th cent. ?) and pasted over some of them. There are
also four of the familiar virgin saints.

Northward lies *Witton*, with some wall-paintings, and west the town
of *North Walsham*. Here the large handsome church has lost its tower.
It has some fine shields (John of Gaunt) in the porch, and has its
painted saints on the screen—none of any rarity. There are two
panels representing the Annunciation, and one obscured by a reading-
desk is a crowned female with a crosier (?) : some people say St.
Wilgefort.

At this point *Worstead* can come in, though it lies south of Walsham.
The manufactures to which it gave its name were removed to Norwich.
But before they went they had raised a noble monument in the shape

of the church, which was begun in 1369. It retains a good deal of noteworthy detail, and the building itself is very fine. In the porch is a boss of the Coronation of the Virgin, treated much as it is in the north cloister at Norwich, with the Virgin kneeling between the Father and the Son.

The splendid screen has been dreadfully repainted : this was last and worst done about 1870 by persons who are conventionally called " worthy." An inscription shows it to have been the work of John Alblastyr and (?) Benedicta his wife in 1512. The panels beginning from the north now show :

Vir doloris, quite modern. Drawings of 1832 or so show that here was a female saint without an attribute. Then follow Paul (formerly Dorothy), James the Less (was Simon), Philip (was Jude with boat), Simon (was William of Norwich (see later)), Jude (was Wilgefort (see later)), Matthias (was Andrew), John (was Peter), Andrew (was James the Great), Peter (was Thomas), Austin (was our Lord blessing), Bartholomew (was John), Jerome (new), William of Norwich un-restored—he has crown of thorns, a dagger in his side, holds two nails and a book. Wilgefort, a woman crowned, bearded, crucified. This lady, a daughter of a king of Portugal, had vowed virginity ; when her father sought to give her in marriage, she prayed that she might become unattractive : a beard grew on her face, and her indignant father crucified her. She goes under many names : Liberata or Livrade in southern countries, in the north Wilgefortis, Ontkommeren or Uncumber. Like the sword of Winfarthing, she would rid wearied wives of their husbands. There is little doubt that the fable was an " ætiological " explanation of the long-robed crowned crucifixes that follow the type of the famous one of Lucca, and are the recognized form of the crucifix in the twelfth century.

There are also side-screens : in the north aisle Bartholomew, Philip with loaves, Lawrence, and Thomas of Canterbury (not, I think, Pope Xystus, as he has been called). At the east end of this aisle note the coloured frame of a retable. Also two loose defaced panels of Peter and Paul. In the south aisle the figures are of Peter and Paul, John Baptist, and Stephen.

A western gallery of 1501 is original, and has a long English inscription on it. There are remains of mural decoration. On a pillar at the south-east is a painted canopy and outline of a figure.

THE PASTON BARN

154

North-east from Walsham is *Edingthorpe*, the church lying apart on a hill-top. The screen is of the fourteenth century, and the paintings of six Apostles, with cusped nimbi, are of good quality.

Then we go to *Bacton*, and in the parish find *Bromholm* priory. Its story is in an introductory chapter. The remains of it, in and about a farmhouse, are certainly worth a visit. We have the gatehouse (Norman below and Perpendicular above), the north transept of the

KNAPTON: THE PISCINA

church (late Norman), the Chapter House, and the undercroft of the dormitory, both of which, being on the east side of the cloister, serve to mark the position and extent of the cloister garth. A good deal of the south wall of the nave of the church is also to be seen. After the arrival of the Rood the choir of the church was much enlarged ; but this part is wholly gone.

At *Paston* there is a fine barn : the manor-house to which it belonged is gone. The wall-paintings in the church were uncovered fairly recently. There is a very good St. Christopher : he wears linen breeches with strings at the knees. Farther east are the three Dead and Three Living, a small figure on right of the latter ; below them a very small kneeling figure, full face, as to the age of which I am left doubtful.

Knapton has one of the most famous roofs in all Norfolk—double hammer-beam, with *three* rows of angels on each side. The lower row of these is not painted : the angels hold the attributes of the Apostles. The second row have shields, and the instruments of the Passion ; the uppermost also shields and some scrolls, one inscribed *Te dominum* from the *Te Deum*. Of the helve-figures the majority are apostles and prophets, one on the south (third from east) is St. Edmund ; several have inscribed scrolls.

There is a very nice angle piscina. The font and cover are late. The font is one of those inscribed with a palindrome in Greek (νιψον ανομημα μη μοναν οψιν), which is one of a set of palindromes composed or collected by the Greek Emperor Leo the Philosopher (*d.* 911) : he called them Crabs.

Trunch has another celebrated nave-roof, with spandrels of open-work to the hammer-beams. Its " baptistery " or font-canopy is, however, its most uncommon feature—a beautiful piece of woodwork. The six panels of the upper stage have all had imagery in them. On the east face was a crucifix with Mary and John in relief, pegged on to the surface. Another Crucifixion occupied the upper half of the field on the north-west face : this also was in relief.

On the screen the panels had the Apostles : their faces have been injured. An inscription on the openings of the northern part of the screen gives the date as 1503 ; that of the southern half is a doxology.

Trimingham, where the cliffs are said to attain a height of 300 ft., is one of a line of coast villages which form a sort of prelude to Cromer. On the rood-screen here are some unfamiliar figures. Besides Edmund, Clement, Barbara, Cecilia, and apparently James, there are Clara with a monstrance and host, one with a palm and perhaps a gridiron, possibly St. Faith, and it seems Jero or Jeron (bearded, wreath on head, hawk on hand, gold armour and red robe) : he is a Flemish saint who was killed by the heathen Normans in 886, and whose relics were at Egmond Abbey. He is invoked for finding lost property.

So on to *Cromer*, which needs no panegyric from me as an attractive place. Its antiquities are not many, but its church (with modern chancel) is a very stately building, with good flint-work and some stone-carving at the west end, which is remarkable. Its old fittings of screens and glass, etc., are gone : they were probably very rich. In 1810 Mr. Britton (or Mr. Evans) wrote of Cromer : " Cromer Bay has the appellation of the *Devil's Throat*. As a watering-place Cromer has attained some celebrity. It is not destitute of comforts ; the adjacent country is picturesque ; and few sea-views can exceed this, which is almost daily crowded with shipping." But I will not linger over it. We have now to turn south, and take stock of some places on and near the road to Aylsham and Norwich. Another excursion will bring us back to the coast west of Cromer.

Felbrigg, besides its woods, has a famous brass in its church, of Sir Simon Felbrigge. The pretty Tudor house is not accessible ; it was

ROUGHTON CHURCH

the home of the famous Windhams. *Roughton* has one of the round towers which are pronounced to be of pre-Conquest date, perhaps even of the tenth century (*Bessingham*, farther west, has another). Then, on the east of the road is *Southrepps*, now without aisles ; the tower is very good. There have been beautiful sedilia ; the heads carved within the south door of the chancel should be noted. A low side-window has a fourteenth-century angel in the glass. At *Anting-*

ham you see (as elsewhere in these counties) two churches in one churchyard. *Suffield* Church does not stand open, as is the laudable custom in most cases ; but if you can get in you find a screen with some unusual figures : Sir John Shorne with his boot and devil ; St. Julian, the Hospitaller ; and others, among whom are recorded Longinus (most unlikely), Jeron, and Louis. At *Colby* is a font with the Evangelists, and also (quite uncommon) the Virgin and Child throned, a man and woman kneeling, a kneeling man with a hatchet over his shoulder, a dog, and a scroll. In the east window, moreover, is old glass : some Apostles, a Cherub standing on his wheel, a Virgin Mary with lily-pot, and a young saint with a palm. At *Erpingham* is a brass of Sir Thomas Erpingham's father. Blomefield saw on the screen here a man kneeling and invoking a child with these words : "Sancte Roberte succurre mihi pie." So St. Robert of Bury had his devotees in Norfolk.

Blickling Hall is famous, and deserves to be. A Hobart built the house (1626), but an earlier one belonged to the Boleyns, and Anne was much here as a child. The views that can be got from a distance are beautiful, and if the house is now shown, of course it should be visited. There is a bridge over the moat, a small forecourt, and then in the main block the splendid staircase. Hear Mr. Blomefield, who describes it as " a curious brick fabric, four-square, with a turret at each corner ; there are two courts, and with the fine library, elegant wilderness, good lake, gardens, and park, it is a pleasant beautiful seat, worthy the observation of such as make the Norfolk tour." Mr. Prebendary Gilpin, about 1780, chimes in : " The moat, the bridges, the turrets, the battlements, are all impressed with the ideas of antiquity. . . . Blickling is now very expensively fitted up, and contains many grand rooms, in which the chimnies, ceilings, wainscot, and other ornaments are in general suitable to the antiquity of the whole." The church merits a visit, particularly from the brass-rubber.

The good town of *Aylsham* would make a convenient centre for exploring much of the country with which I have been dealing. Like Cromer it is " not destitute of comforts," and it is very pretty in itself. The handsome church has the lower part of a screen dated 1507 with Apostles and two Prophets. South of the chancel is a fine figure of St. John in sixteenth-century foreign glass.

Christopher Layer, the Jacobite, who was executed for high treason in 1722, was an Aylsham man. There is a tablet to his memory on a house in the town.

On this particular route we will confine ourselves to what lies *east* of the Aylsham–Norwich road. *Burgh-next-Aylsham* has a remarkably fine Early English chancel, arcaded, and a Seven Sacraments font. On the eighth (south-east) panel is a man kneeling at a vested altar with a broken chalice on it. The scene of Confession has the re-treating devil ; round the base are four Prophets.

At *Oxnead*, remains of a fine hall built by Sir Clement Paston, a n d Paston monuments in the church. *Marsham*, on the main road, has a screen a good deal damaged and repainted. T h e figures are all Apostles, except two—a bishop, and a woman holding a saw who is taken to be St. Faith. She more usually holds a hook or a gridiron, but at Horsham has the saw. This is one of three churches hard by

AYLSHAM: FONT PANEL WITH THE LION OF ST. MARK

in which Blomefield records a great quantity of old glass, heraldry filling the clerestory, and many single figures of saints. The font had the Seven Sacraments and eight figures of saints, including St. George.

The other two churches in question are *Buxton* and *Lammas*. At the latter was a whole window with the Last Judgment and four of the Works of Mercy, performed by a woman, and with rhymes in English. At *Buxton* was another elaborate window, of the Assumption and possibly the other Joys of the Virgin, with many scrolls. All gone. *Stratton Strawless*, where the Marsham monuments are good, was almost as rich. In a north-east window was a great Coronation of the Virgin, and below SS. Katherine and Margaret and donors (Marshams). The end of Blomefield's note is sadly worth transcribing : " When I was here April 10 1732 all the effigies but one were here, but the 3 lights of the lower parts of the panes being new glazed since, they are all gone, with the inscriptions ; but the rest of the window still remains perfect." I fear it does not now.

Coltishall and *Horstead* are both pretty places in this region, Horstead Mill being particularly attractive. We can revert to the main road and end this excursion with *Horsham St. Faith*. Here was a not incon-siderable Benedictine priory founded in 1105 by Robert de Caen. The site adjoins the churchyard on the north, and is now in a private house and garden. The garden seems to coincide with the cloister-garth ; there is a rich doorway in the north-east corner. A wall-painting of the Crucifixion was formerly to be seen within, but perished in a fire not long ago ; fortunately, it had been copied by Professor Tristram. It was a fine work of the thirteenth century. The church has a Norman door and two pieces of interesting painting. (I) The screen : it is late, being dated 1528, the gift of William Wulcy and his wives Joan and Alice. Reckoning from the left we have : (1) a Dominican nun, " St. Katherine of Siena " ; (2) crowned lady, holding a burning heart—perhaps this is really St. Katherine ; (3) nun with book ; (4) man in armour with sword pointing upwards ; (5) crowned, with cross and book ; (6) a bishop with crosier and perhaps an auger—if so, St. Leger ; (7) (on south) St. Brigida—seated nun with open book ; Christ appearing on a cloud ; (8) St. Oswaldus as king, with book ; (9) St. Apollonia with forceps and tooth ; (10) beardless, in red cloak ; (11) St. Genevieve (?)—a lady with candle and what looks like a boat ; (12) St. Anna, but she is wreathed and holds flames. Authorities say that St. Wandregisil (a Norman abbot) is here, but I did not detect him. (II) The pulpit, dated 1480. On the panels of this are painted : (1) (north-east) Virgin and Child ; St. Faith crowned, with saw and book ; a clerk with a scroll inscribed

in English beginning " Blisful lady marie of hevyn borne. . . ." (West);
St. Thomas of Canterbury as archbishop, blessing ; St. Christopher
(South-west), St. Andrew, St. John Evangelist (South), St. John Bap-
tist, St. Stephen.

Thus much for *North-east Norfolk*.
We will now take—

MID-NORTH NORFOLK

This district we can perhaps deal
with most effectively by starting
out on the road or rail leading to
Cawston, eventually making Wells
and Holkham our north-westerly
limit, and returning by Fakenham.
Cawston is the first church I notice.
The building is magnificent, and
is cruciform in plan. The double
hammer-beam roof, one of the most
noted of its kind, has a cornice of
cherubins, and six-winged angels
stand on the hammer-beams. Much
of the seating is old — backless
benches with popeys. In the south
transept is a painting on the east
wall, very hard to decipher, said
to represent the dedication of the
church to St. Agnes. We see a
large crowned figure seated ; on left
is a door with a ring ; on each
side of the central figure is another

CAWSTON: ALMS-BOX

person holding a long scroll in-
scribed in English ; there are traces of other figures. I seemed to
read " Mary heven queene " on the right-hand scroll ; but I have not
seen a full decipherment.

Cawston screen is most remarkable. The figures from left are :
(1) St. Agnes, the beginning of an English inscription below, " *pray
for the* " ; (2) St. Helena with double cross : then Apostles—Thomas,
John, James the Great, Andrew, Paul, Peter (his book inscribed

11

perhaps with *Quod* (*autem*) *habeo hoc* (*tibi do*) from Acts iii. These figures form one of three sets by different artists (as distinguished by Col. Strange ; see *Walpole Society*, vol. for 1912–13). Then come the doors which, as almost always, have the Four Doctors—Gregory, Jerome (as cardinal, with lion), Ambrose, Augustine. A new feature is that on the edge of the doors are small figures in black and gold under arches—Katherine, Angel, George and Dragon, Angel. South of the doors are first two figures by the same hand as the Doctors—Matthias and Bartholomew ; then a third group of finer work, in which the figures are on parchment cut out to the shape and fastened to the wood—Philip with loaves, Jude with boat, James the Less with club, Simon in spectacles, and something beside him that looks like a log and chain, Matthew with halbert. Last of all Sir John Shorne, a cap on his head, holding a boot with the devil's head emerging. It has been observed that some of the cartoons for the apostles have been used at Marsham (and Worstead), and that the gesso patterns are identical with some at Marsham and Aylsham.

There were fine windows in the south transept, of the Creation, Deluge, Passion, etc., in Blomefield's time. Little enough now, but among some fragments of glass preserved at the parsonage is one with the name of St. Blida (mother of St. Walstan, as recorded earlier).

A detour south-west will take us to *Booton*, where the excellent writer, Whitwell Elwin (long editor of the *Quarterly Review*), was incumbent, and spent enormous care and much money upon rebuilding his church. I believe we should admire and applaud him more than it ; it has two very odd towers at the west end ; but I have never seen it. Westward is *Reepham*, which once had *three* parish churches in one churchyard, and still has two. In that of *Reepham* proper is a splendid tomb effigy (of 1337) of Sir Roger de Kerdiston. The figure, rather like that at Ingham, is conceived (say Pryor and Gardiner) " as laid on a stony bed, bivouacking on the battlefield." There are eight good figures of mourners in relief on the front of the tomb. There are also brasses here. Northward lies *Sall*, a very famous church, recalling perhaps its neighbour Cawston, but richer. It has an aisled nave of six bays with two porches, transepts, chancel, and western tower (note the feathered censing angels in the spandrels of the doorway). When I first saw this church, in 1884, it needed a great deal of repair, and this it has had, thanks to kind benefactors, and the work has been well done. Pages might be written on the glass and carving and painting here, but I cannot inflict the whole of my notes on the reader. The north porch has a fine stone boss of the Last Judgment in its roof. Entering, you will note the old ringers' gallery in the tower. From it projects a carved and painted bracket with an apparatus for drawing up the font cover (a good specimen). The font itself has the Seven Sacraments and the Cruci-

REEPHAM: WEEPERS ON TOMB OF SIR ROGER DE KERDISTON

fixion (with the Virgin swooning). The base is inscribed, and has the name of the donor Thomas Line. The nave roof is powdered with *Ihs's* and crowned M's. On the cornice (from north-west) can be read part of the 150th Psalm with the Gloria, and great part of the *Te Deum*. Over the chancel arch is an ancient canopy. The transept roofs are all but flat and exquisitely panelled.

The lower part only of the screen remains, and the figures on it

SALL: THE FONT

are damaged. The Apostles' C r e e d, much of it, can be read on the upper edge ; each panel had two Apostles. Thomas and James the Less were most easily distinguished on the northern half. The doors have the Four Doctors ; on the south P h i l i p (with long cross) and Bartholomew were to be seen.

The chancel roof is a most beautiful specimen. The central bosses, of wood, have these subjects, reckoning from the west : Annunciation, Nativity and Shepherds, Presentation, Adoration of t h e Magi, Entry into J e r u s a l e m, L a s t Supper, Crucifixion, Resurrection, Ascension.

Of glass there has been a great deal of admirable quality, chiefly confined to the tracery lights ; much of it has been shifted into other windows since I recorded it; but it will be no bad thing to set down what was the original arrangement. In the east window tracery were the Nine Orders of Angels—possibly two figures for each order. Beginning from left were : two *Archangeli*, then two *Principatus* with devils at their feet. Then two *Dominations*, also with devils (but the name is gone). Higher up a *Seraph* (name only), and two *Potestates* with red dragons ; besides other angels with shields. The north and south chancel windows had patriarchs and prophets in the tracery ; also two cardinals. The east window of the south transept had the Annunciation (in two lights), and virgin saints (Barbara, Dorothy, Margaret, Katherine), one bishop, and a man and two women (donors) saying *Nos cum prole pia Benedicat virgo Maria*. The south window of this transept had several musician angels, and St. Giles, Etheldreda, Vincent with flesh-hook (now moved), and Helena. In the north transept (south-east window) were angels and a figure of the Virgin from a Coronation ; in the next window northwards Mercy and Truth (gone) and Righteousness and Peace meeting, with the appropriate psalm-verse. A little more glass was in a south nave window. I reckoned this glass to be as fine as any in Norfolk, especially the Orders in the east window. When the main lights of the windows were filled there must have been a very glorious show.

Heydon, a little to the north, had a wonderful window, very elaborately described by Blomefield. It represented Christ covered with wounds, and the Virgin, and round these a number of groups of men dicing, drinking, and so forth, and swearing by all the members of Christ's body, which they thereby wound. A painting of the same subject is in Broughton Church, Bucks. Nothing is left at Heydon, but I mention it partly because it is chronicled in Nelson's *Ancient Painted Glass* as still extant.

There is or was a painted screen of 1520 (with donors on it) at *Edgefield* ; and east of this is *Plumstead* (panels of screen) and then *Matlask* (popey-heads) and the *Barninghams*. The front of the Jacobean Hall at Barningham Winter—a Paston house—is a famous example, and at Barningham Northwood there is a wheel-cross pattern in the floor of the church which has excited curiosity : unseen by me.

We turn west to Holt and pass *Baconsthorpe*, with Heydon monuments in the church, and an Easter sepulchre, and also a Hall of Tudor date ;

and so to *Holt*, famous for its native Sir Thomas Gresham (*b.* 1507), and for his foundation of Gresham's School, which thrives greatly under the patronage of the Fishmongers.

The north coast and *Sheringham* are no distance away. The attractions of Sheringham are on the surface : it commands a pleasant and interesting country. The church of Upper Sheringham has something of a screen, but better things in this line are to be seen if we follow the

coast westward, all among the salt marshes with high ground rising on our left.

Beeston Regis, however, a little east of Sheringham, must not be forgotten. The Augustinian priory has left some remains—the west end of a cruciform church ; the Chapter House also can be traced. In the parish church are portions of a screen (not *in situ*) and a good roof.

CLEY: PANEL OF FONT—" EXTREME UNCTION "

At *Weybourne* another Augustinian priory—tower and east window of the church remain. Weybourne harbour was anciently thought to be a very vulnerable point for invasions. After this we come to *Salthouse* ; the church, rather desolate, stands well. It has the remains of painted screens made into pews. Several Apostles, and some other saints are readily decipherable.

Cley has a very notable church, once cruciform or meant to be, but with transepts in ruins. The unusual clerestory, with a mixture of ordinary and circular windows, should be noted. Also the porch with heraldry of Richard II's time. Stalls with misericords are in the chancel, and there are brasses of some importance, but no paintings or glass.

Blakeney Church is a great land and sea mark. The pretty, slender tower that rises at the northeast of the chancel and seems meant for a beacon at once attracts attention. The main west tower is a fine one. Another rarity here besides the supplementary tower is the *vaulted* Early English chancel. Great care has been taken of this church of late years, and some of the modern furnishing is very good. The nave has its old hammer-beam roof. There is some little glass collected into one window, including a Resurrection. In this parish are the remains of a Carmelite friary. Of the bird sanctuary, and the fascination of the marshes about here, much has been written.

CLEY CHURCH: LABEL STOP

After *Morston* (screen panels with the Evangelists and the Doctors), a little detour southward is advisable to include *Field Dalling* (glass : Apostles in tracery lights, and *perhaps* wall-paintings), and in particular *Binham*, where the nave of the priory church is one of the best of Norfolk monuments.

The house was a cell to St. Albans Abbey, and was always quarrelling with it. The chief feature in its obscure history was when Robert Fitzwalter about 1210 besieged it (because the Abbot of St. Albans had removed the Prior of Binham, who was a friend of Fitzwalter).

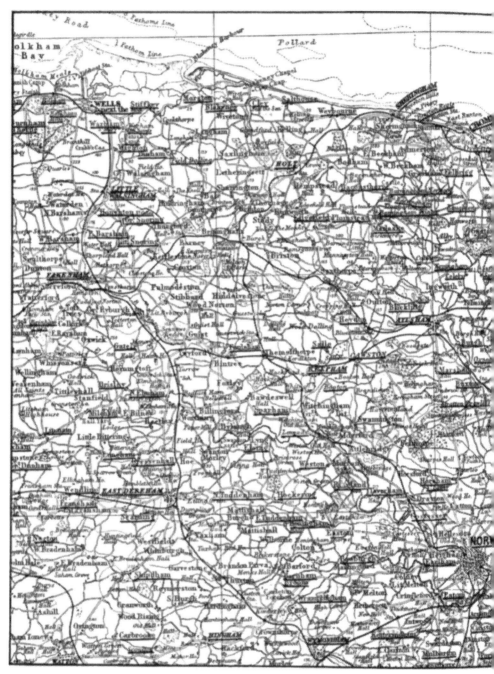

SCALE ¼″—1 MILE

EAST

BINHAM PRIORY: PART OF THE WEST FRONT

" By God's feet," said King John when he heard of it, " either I or Fitzwalter must be king in England," and he sent men and raised the siege. At the Dissolution the annual value was £140 to £150. We enter the precinct by the " Jail Gate," south-west of the church : it is a thirteenth-century building. The church then fronts us. It has a noble Early English façade, which replaced the original Norman one, perhaps after the siege. And we find that the building now consists of the seven westernmost bays of the Norman nave, terminated at the east by a wall built on the original stone *pulpitum* or screen. The aisles of the nave have been cut off, and are ruinous ; the arcade has been built up. The researches of Harrod, supplemented by the very interesting ones of Dr. Fairweather (see Ingleby, *Supplement*, p. 324), have furnished a key to the original plan. The transepts and choir of the church are reduced to complete ruin. The transepts had apsidal chapels on the east, and the choir ended originally in three apses, but appears to have been (as in other cases) enlarged eastwards and made square-ended. A similar thing happened to the Chapter House (only here the apse seems to have been cut off). The cloister was on the south.

The remaining fragment of the church, which was probably from the first the parish church, is most remarkable. It contains some good seats with open-work backs, and the lower panels of the screen, which now stand east and west, have been painted over with texts, and whitewashed ; but the figures are still discernible, though not all identifiable. Reckoning from the east we have : (1) young man in gold armour ; (2) bishop in gold cope ; (3) Alban holding a peculiar cross with a disc on the top. This, please note, is the correct attribute of St. Alban : it was the cross given to him by Amphibalus who converted him ; and he held it in his hands when he was beheaded. It strayed in after years to London, but was recovered by the Abbey (about 1230), and preserved there as a great relic ; (4) beardless, in gold robes, perhaps holding a gold horn ; (5) a lady ; (6) a king ; (7) (?) Helena with a cross ; (8) Christopher ; (9 and 10) nothing ; (11) possibly Mary of Egypt ; (12) Henry VI standing on an antelope ; (13) holding a rich gold cross ; (14) has a jug and towel near ; (15) Katherine ; (16) Michael. The font has the Seven Sacraments and Baptism of Christ, and round the base are Apostles.

The curious low transom in the west windows of the aisles is a consequence of the remodelling of the west end, when the earlier vaulting of the aisles was destroyed.

If we now revert to the coast we shall hit *Stiffkey* (*alias* Stewkey), and pass a very beautiful towered house built by Sir Nicholas Bacon, but probably not to be explored. Then comes *Wells-next-the-Sea*, which makes a good centre for these regions, and once had a fine church. Indeed, it still has ; but there is little in it that is old, for it was burnt out—struck by lightning—in the dreadful August of 1879.

The splendid park and house of *Holkham* are hard by. The house — of 1734–60—is a famous one of its kind. It is indeed very grandiose, but it suffers outside from being built of white brick, which unluckily came into fashion and caught the Earl of Leicester's fancy when he was planning to build. I can always read with pleasure the praises lavished by our ancestors on these great seats. "There may be houses," say Messrs. Britton-Evans, "larger and more magnificent, and in some more uniformity and justness of proportion may be visible ; but human

WARHAM ST. MARY: DETAIL OF WINDOW IN NAVE

genius could not contrive anything in which convenience could be more apparent than it is in this. . . . The marble chimney-pieces are all handsome . . . (one) in the State bedrooms representing two pelicans, is exceedingly chaste and beautiful," with much more. Special permission, I may note, is needed to obtain access to the house.

At present we go no farther west, but make southward for Norwich. And first we come to the *Warhams*. Warham Camp, lying south of the villages, is a well-marked earthwork called Danish. Both churches are worth looking at. In All Saints' are brasses and a stone figure in the chancel, of early date. In St. Mary's is a good deal of glass, English and foreign, principally the latter. The east window has : Betrayal, Deposition, Burial ; Christ bidding farewell to the Virgin (uncommon, this) ; Entry into Jerusalem ; Transfiguration. In a south-east window is sixteenth-century foreign glass, a large King David, part of a scene with John Baptist, heads of a Cistercian abbot and monks. In a south chancel window an inscription of 1628 naming German donors ; bits of lettering indicating scenes or types of the Passion. In a north nave window groups of Dominicans and Cistercians. Next to *Wighton*, where is another earthwork, Crabb's Castle, and, it seems, some glass ; also saints on the lower panels of the screen and a wall-painting are recorded— not seen by me. Then we are at *Walsingham*, Great and Little, or Old and New, of which Old or Great Walsingham is to the north. But interest is concentrated on New Walsingham. Of the Priory the story has been told. The remains are in private grounds (accessible usually on Wednesdays).

The plan elicited by Harrod in 1853 shows a very long church without transepts, and cloister garth on the south. It is possible that the *Santa Casa* chapel and its covering building were attached to the north side of the nave, but no undoubted remains can be pointed out. The east end of the church is left, with its adjoining stair turrets, and a small round window above the main east window. Bases of the columns at the west end have also been uncovered. In the refectory, south of the cloister-garth, the pulpit in the side wall may be seen, and also the west window, and the buttery hatch. Some way east of the church are two wells (wishing wells), and by them a late Norman arch, removed from some other part of the buildings.

LITTLE WALSINGHAM: CONDUIT IN THE "COMMON PLACE"

The precinct is entered by a fifteenth-century gatehouse, which has a jocose representation of a man looking out of a small window. An interesting stone-roofed conduit stands in the " Common Place," and there are picturesque old houses in the town.

As we emerge from it on the south, on the right side of the road are the very considerable remains of the Franciscan friary, founded in the fourteenth century by Elizabeth de Burgh Countess of Clare.

HOUGHTON ST. GILES: THE "SLIPPER CHAPEL"

The buildings are occupied as a farm. The best-preserved piece is a small cloister court, where much of the window tracery survives. A large building running north and south has its two gables ; it had a floor half-way up. The plan of the church is not very clear. In the parish church the font with the Seven Sacraments and Crucifixion is notable, and there is some little glass, very much pieced, in the chancel windows.

EAST BARSHAM: THE MANOR-HOUSE

Next comes *Houghton St. Giles*, or *H.-in-the-dale*. The screen in the church here has to be examined. It has twelve figures, the names written on the sill above. Those on the north are a set we have not yet met with : (1) a woman, nimbed, in a Jewish cap, and a nimbed boy. The name above is hardly legible. It was probably meant for Anna : it should in fact be Emeria (which occurs later over the undoubted picture of Anne). Emeria is not familiar here, but in the Netherlands she was, and was said to be the sister of Anne and ancestress of St. Servatius of Maestricht, who is probably the boy here : also mother of Elizabeth. We find Emeria or Hismeria in the early German paintings of the Holy Family (die Heilige Sippe). (2) S. Maria Salome (the mother of James and John, who are here with staff and cup). (3) S. Maria Cleophe, with her four sons. (4) S. Maria : the Virgin crowned and the Child. (5) S. Elysabeth, and John Baptist with lamb. (6) S. Emeria, really Anne, teaching the Virgin to read (No. 1 has usually been called S. Monica, but there is no precedent for this). South of the door we have : (7) S. Gregorius papa, as pope. (8) S. Jeronimus cardinalis. (9) S. Ambrosius episcopus. (10) S. Augustinus episcopus. (11) S. Silvester papa with a suppliant lady who says *Silvester sancte me tua salva prece.* (12) S. Clemens papa. All the faces, and the word papa, have been scratched. The former coving of the screen, at top, is traceable.

Then, not far off on the lower road, near the line, is the very beautiful Slipper Chapel, or Shoe Chapel, where it was said pilgrims took off their shoes and walked the last two miles to Walsingham barefoot. It is a charming fourteenth-century building : the window tracery, pinnacles, niches, buttresses, all admirable. Of late years it has been purchased for the Benedictine Order and repaired, and is very well cared for.

The wonderful brick Hall of *East Barsham* can be well seen from the road. It is of late fifteenth and early sixteenth centuries, built by Sir William Fermor ; then it passed to the Calthorpes, and then to the Lestranges. In front of the main building stands the roofless gatehouse with the royal arms over the gate in moulded brick. The house has splendid bands of ornament in moulded brick, and turrets and chimneys, which, with other details, are figured in many an architectural text-book.

12

GREAT SNORING RECTORY

The church of *West Barsham* has Norman portions and an alabaster relief of the Adoration of the Magi. East lies *Great Snoring*. In the church the screen has been to a very slight extent cleared of a coat of paint, but no figures are visible. A mutilated Shelton brass of 1423 has some enamelled heraldry. In the tracery of the beautiful fourteenth-century east window seem to have been Angels ; in a south chancel window several of the Orders remain : (1) six-winged with viol ; (2) feathered, with balances ; (3) crowned and armed ; (4) *Dominaciones* with sceptre ; (5) *Cherubin*; (6) Angel with scroll of *Sanctus*. There is an unwontedly early table of the Commandments with flanking pictures of the Four Last Things—Death, Judgment, Heaven, and Hell. The royal arms are also old : the initials I(acobus) R(ex) and date 1608 may have been added. The motto is *Quae Deus coniunxit nemo separet.* Supporters, lion and unicorn. The sedilia (14th cent.) are beautiful, and so is a piscina in the south aisle : it has admirable foliage ; a carving of a six-winged angel is by it. Notice a band of panelling at the base of the east wall, with shields. Is it the side of a tomb ?

The Rectory, visible from the churchyard, was built by Sir Ralph Shelton (*temp.* Henry VII). It has polygonal turrets and a band of quatrefoils, etc., in squares running all along the west front which is stuccoed ; the south end is not stuccoed, and is the most beautiful part. It is a reminder of East Barsham.

In *Little Snoring* Church there is a good deal of Norman work. The round tower stands south-west of the present church, and has a Norman arch and the outline of the gable of a nave attached to it on the east side. The south door is very remarkable. The font is early : notice the very wide-splayed lancets at the east end and the piscina. The royal arms here have the date 1686.

Fakenham Church is imposing, but does not contain much except the fine fourteenth-century sedilia and some brasses. Parts of the screen seem to be of the fourteenth century. Some way to the west is the great house of *Houghton*, finished by Sir Robert Walpole in 1735. (He and Horace are buried in the church.) In the opinion of Mr. Britton or his colleague, Houghton and Holkham " fill the mind with everything that magnificence can inspire." We have heard of the sale of the pictures to Catherine of Russia, and know how it enraged Horace Walpole. The church has in it a good effigy of a prior of

Cokesford. *East Rudham* might be inserted here, for in the parish are the ruins of Cokesford priory (Augustinian), consisting of the

LITTLE SNORING CHURCH

north wall of the church and a window. In the parish church there are remains of Nottingham alabaster sculptures, representing the

Annunciation, Crucifixion, Coronation of the Virgin, St. Anthony with his pig, St. John in the cauldron of oil, and St. John Baptist. South-west of Fakenham is another great house—that of the Town-sends—*Raynham*. This dates from 1630, a work of Inigo Jones. The park is large ; the house not shown.

Taking the Norwich road we have first to turn off to *Gateley* (key of church in village). There is some good old seating here, and the screen, which has been repainted, has a very odd collection of figures : their names are added in careful but not very intelligent reproduction of the old lettering. From left they are : (1) S. Audria (Etheldreda) as abbess ; (2) S. Elisabetha, arms crossed on breast ; (3) S. Maria the Virgin, hand on breast (these two perhaps making a group of the Visitation) ; (4) Sancta Puella Ridibowne, a girl in a black habit with a book and a spray of flowers, who cannot be satisfactorily accounted for. (South) (5) Called St. Louis in the books—seemed to me to be a Pope in a green cope, with a patriarchal (double) cross and a book in a chemise-cover ; (6) Rex Henricus VI with sceptre, orb, and closed crown, in red mantle ; (7) Sanctus [illegible], a bishop in cope with crosier and book, guessed to be St. Augustine ; (8) Magister Iohannes Schorn in cap and red habit, with boot and devil in it.

We might then either go east to *Foulsham* (the church is fine and has brasses and some glass) or continue south to *Brisley*. A rather early Christopher on the *south* wall is flanked by smaller figures of Andrew and (?) Bartholomew. There is much fine old seating. Is the pulpit of the " three-decker " mediæval ? The screen is good, but has no pictures. The sedilia are nice. Under the chancel is a sacristy, quite plain.

North Elmham claims attention. The site of its cathedral lying north of the parish church was investigated, and the plan described by Messrs. A. W. Clapham and W. H. Godfrey (see the *Antiquaries Journal*, 1926, iv, 402). The church stood in the south-west angle of a large earthwork, and, late in the fourteenth century, the Bishop of Norwich (Henry Despencer) turned the derelict remains of it into a fortified manor-house, which itself fell to ruins after the sixteenth century. To our eyes the church would have looked rather strange and exotic. It consisted of a massive west tower leading into a nave of the same breadth, then into a transept, then into a short apse : in the angles of transepts and nave were two more towers. Practically, the plan is a Tau cross, with a slight semi-circular projection at the east end : the whole hardly 100 ft. long. The extant walls are nowhere high enough to give any idea of the windows, and there is really no ornamental detail left. But it is a venerable monument of the Anglo-Saxon church.

The parish church has several features of interest. In the west porch a boss of the Coronation of the Virgin. In several north aisle windows are remains of fourteenth-century glass : (1) Angel with psaltery ; (2) beautiful branches and foliage ; (3) crowned Virgin and Child ; (4) more foliage.

The screen panels now number eighteen ; older accounts tell of a few more which have disappeared. They are—(1) left, St. Benedict ; (2) another abbot ; (3) blank ; (4) Thomas (?) ; (5) with sword and hind at his feet—has been called Giles wrongly : Henry VI is suggested with more probability by Dom Camm ; but why no crown ? ; (6) Jude, boat ; (7) Camm says James the Less—I noted him as Andrew ; (8) Philip, loaves ; (9) John, with cup and dragon ; (10) Paul. The doors, which had the Four Doctors, are gone. The south : (11) Barbara, tower ; (12) Cecilia, her head wreathed with lilies and holding a wreath ; (13) Dorothy, flowers ; (14) Sitha, kerchief and rosary ; (15) Juliana, devil in chain ; (16) Petronilla, key and book—she only has the key because of being St. Peter's daughter ; (17) Agnes, a sword-point in her throat, holding a lamb ; (18) Cristina, two arrows in her body. The rest blank.

South-east to *Elsing*, " perhaps the finest Decorated church in Norfolk," certainly admirable. Its font cover has its original paint and gold : some modern apostle-figures have been added. In the south chancel windows are remains of a series of Apostles bearing clauses of the Creed (late 14th or early 15th cent.) : Jude and James the Less are distinct. The screen panels are faint ; they have : (left) Katherine, Dorothy, two figures forming the Visitation— Anne and the Virgin, Michael, George, John Evangelist, and John Baptist. There is record of wall-paintings of the fourteenth century, representing " events in the life of John Baptist," but these are invisible. That for which Elsing is best known is the great brass of Sir Hugh Hastings, the builder of the church ; it is flanked by bands containing small effigies of his friends, under canopies, several of which have disappeared. One, indeed, made its way to the Fitz-

WALSOKEN CHURCH.

CASTLE RISING; INTERIOR OF KEEP.

william Museum at Cambridge, and was gladly bought (by me) ; but when its provenance was recognized it was returned to the church. In view of such perils the brass is now protected by a locked cover and hidden from sight.

Elsing Hall is a venerable moated house, but I do not know that it is shown.

Rejoin the main road and come to *Sparham*. Here are two pairs of panels from the screen, now set up in the north aisle. They seem to me very late, particularly the first pair. These show : (1) the inside of a church. In the foreground a shrouded skeleton-corpse stands in a grave in the floor. On left is a font with a fine cover ; a scroll says *fuissem quasi non essem* ; a second scroll, *De utero* ; a third, held by the corpse, *Translatus ad tumulum. Job* 10 (the text is in fact Job x. 19). (2) Two skeleton-corpses of a man and woman, fully dressed. The man has a torch, round which is a scroll *sic transit gloria mundi* ; the woman has a bunch of flowers. Scrolls above have this couplet :

> *Natus homo de muliere brevi de tempore parvo*
> *Nunc est nunc non est quasi flos qui crescit in arvo.*

These are quite abnormal subjects to find on a screen. They are not a Dance of Death, but a *Memento mori*. The second pair of panels have a good picture of St. Walstan, crowned and robed, with sceptre and scythe, and his oxen at his feet, and St. Thomas of Canterbury, with his archiepiscopal pallium, blessing. There are relics of seating in the church and an ancient pulpit.

As we pass *Lenwade* and, at no great distance, *Weston*, let us remember with gratitude the Rev. James Woodforde and his Diary, and Mr. John Beresford, who brought it to light, and has already edited four volumes of calm delightful reading.

Screens with figures are recorded at *Ringland* and *Taverham*, and wall-paintings and a fragment of one of Sir John Fastolf's houses at *Drayton*. *Costessey* (Cossey), the old seat of the Jerninghams, has their monuments in its church, and a screen.

We are now back at Norwich, which, when we have left it once more by the Dereham road, will cease to be our centre. For we now have to deal with, first the belt of country on either side of the Dereham–Swaffham–Lynn road, and then use Lynn for a centre and go north and south from it.

MID AND WEST NORFOLK

On the road to East Dereham there is something in the way of monuments and seating to be seen at *Honingham, Hockering,* and *East Tuddenham* ; but at *North Tuddenham* there is more—the church stands prettily. It has been defaced inside with tiresome painting, but has retained glass and screen. The glass is not small in amount, but needs more deciphering than I was able to give it. Three panels at the base of the west window I thought referred to St. Agnes. On the left she is seen with her lamb—there is an inscribed scroll beginning *miserere* ; in the centre she is seen again, and a man falling back. It may be the scene of her being sent to a house of ill fame, and a youth miraculously repulsed ; the third is a meeting of two persons with scrolls.

Most of the nave windows have figures in the tracery lights : Nelson's book names SS. Bartholomew, Blida, Edward Confessor, Edmund, Lawrence, and James the Great. I did not discern all of these. In the tower are screen-panels—possibly of the Evangelists and Doctors : certainly Matthew, Ambrose, Augustine. The panels of the rood-screen have been repainted. From north we have : two blanks ; Agnes with sword at throat and lamb at feet ; Dorothy ; probably Jeron with hawk on hand ; Katherine ; (?) Sebastian in red cap, mantle, girt with sword, holding an arrow ; Etheldreda ; Roch, red mantle, hat on shoulder, high loose boots, holding staff and showing his plague sore. His presence makes Sebastian probable (who is otherwise not at all common in England), for these are the two great plague-saints.

And then *East Dereham,* where we think of Cowper, who died and was buried here in 1800, and of George Borrow, who was born at Dumpling Green, south of the town, in 1803, and has much to say of " pretty D——," in the early pages of *Lavengro.* The town is indeed pleasant, and the church and churchyard sloping away to the west, with the massive detached bell-tower, are not easily forgotten. There is less Perpendicular work in it than in most that we have seen. The chancel is Early English, the nave and south aisle mid thirteenth century, the north aisle fourteenth. There are transepts with eastern chapels, which have old painted ceilings. That of St. Thomas of Canterbury is diapered with crowns and T's, that of St. James with

EAST DEREHAM

double-headed eagles. There was originally a central tower, but about 1500 a " new clocker " was built in the churchyard. The font is of 1468, and an extant bill shows that it cost £12 13s. 9d., of which £10 was the cost of the carving. It has the Seven Sacraments in this order : *east* face, Eucharist ; *south-east,* Orders ; *south,* Marriage ; *south-west,* Extreme Unction ; *west,* Crucifixion, with Mary, John, and other figures ; *north-west,* Baptism ; *north,* Confirmation ; *north-east,* Penance with man kneeling at a bench, angel, and devil. Round the base are figures of eight Apostles, and above them Evangelists. There is a noteworthy old chest found at Buckenham Castle, and given in 1786.

Of St. Withburga and her well I have already written.

From Dereham a small round may be made. First to *Gressenhall* (key at the rectory, some little way off). The lower stage of the tower is Norman, and the church is cruciform. There are screen panels with SS. Leonard and Augustine practically effaced and Gregory almost ; then Michael and the Dragon ; angels above. The ceiling of the south transept is fine, with large cruciform paterae. The sedilia are interesting : into the wall at the back of them are built some curiously patterned slabs, one like a square maze with a central shield, and on the top is placed a bit of a sculpture of the stoning of Stephen. Note a fine double arch in the west face of the tower, and a piece of Norman sculpture built in. Then by *Longham* (screen) and *Mileham* (some glass and Coke monuments) to *Litcham.* Here the tower is of brick, and there are still box-pews : also a fine chest. The screen has to be noticed in detail. On the north half are all female saints, much effaced : I can make nothing certain of Nos. 1–5 ; (6) is Petronilla, with book and key ; (7) may have a crosier ; (8) is Ursula with an arrow in each hand, and virgins kneeling at her feet. On the south we have (1) (?) Gregory ; (2) Edmund ; (3) a figure as yet not met with, viz. Armagilus or Armel, in chasuble over armour, leading a dragon by a stole round its neck. He is a Breton, from whom Ploërmel is named, and I was once told by that great scholar, Henry Bradshaw, that Henry VII as Earl of Richmond was in peril of shipwreck off the Breton coast and was told to invoke St. Armagilus, which doing he was delivered. Hence a devotion to St. Armagilus, which is attested by various images and prayer-books of Henry VII's time, e.g. a statue in Henry VII's Chapel, another on Cardinal

GREAT SNORING CHURCH ; SEDILIA.

SOUTH LOPHAM.

Morton's tomb at Canterbury, a painting at Romsey ; (4) Jeron with hawk on hand ; (5) Walstan with crown, sceptre, and scythe ; (6) Eustace kneeling with bow and hounds in leash : a white stag with crucifix between its antlers, on left ; (7) William of Norwich with a knife and three nails, much damaged ; (8) a crowned female in ermine cloak holding nails. On the doors were six figures. Apparently the right figure on the south door was Jerome. The pulpit is old.

We can go from Litcham to *Great Dunham,* where there is pre-Conquest work in the nave of the church, or else through the *Lexhams,* where the last Great Bustard was killed in 1838, and make for *Castle Acre.* Here three buildings attract us. Least of the three the castle of the de Warrennes—of William de Warrenne, the great noble who founded the Cluniac Priory of Lewes and with his wife Gundrada lay there till their coffins (still to be seen at Lewes, in Southover Church) were dug up by railway makers. The man was of great note in his day, but there is not very much left of his castle. The large earthwork in which it stands is thought to be older than the eleventh century, and Roman remains have been found there. Second comes the parish church, large and spacious. In it we note first the tall delicate font cover with pelican at the top, which has been repainted. There are wooden arches across the aisles—remnants of parcloses. The pulpit is composed of painted panels, representing the Four Doctors. Each has an inscribed scroll and all are seated : Augustine has *Impletus spiritus sancto predicavit* ; Gregory : *Gloria predicantium est profectus audientium* ; Jerome : *Ne te decipiat sermonis pulcritudo* ; Ambrose : *Evangelium mentes omnium rigat.* Of the screen the lower panels only are left, well painted with the Apostles, and Christ with book, blessing. The piscina was fine, and had a canopy now hacked off ; there are stalls in the chancel, and some fragments of glass in the east window of the south aisle—a knight (St. George ?), a lamb, a king, etc.

Most remarkable of all is the third, the Priory, than which no finer ruin is to be found in Norfolk. It is approached through the ancient gatehouse which leads into a meadow sloping down to the stream of the Nar. De Warrenne founded it in 1085 as a cell to Lewes, and so it was a Cluniac house.

The west front of the church (adjoined by the very picturesque late prior's lodging, to which we shall return) is all (except a large Perpendicular window inserted in it) of fine Norman work very richly arcaded.   It was flanked by two towers, flush with the front, of which the southern one has survived in part.   The nave was of seven bays, with aisles ; the transepts each had an apsidal eastern chapel.   The choir and both its aisles were also originally apsidal, but in the fourteenth century were lengthened and made square-ended : we have often seen this in other churches of the kind.

Of the cloister on the south all the arcades are gone.   The apsidal Chapter House opened directly out of it on the east.   The dormitory runs southward from this, with its vaulted undercroft ; and at the south end is the well-preserved *necessarium* running east and west, over the drain.   The refectory lies along the south of the cloister. Of the infirmary little is left.   It lay to the east of the cloister-garth. An excellent plan of the whole site is on view on the spot.   The Prior's Lodging is a very pretty piece of late Perpendicular building with a charming bay window, and in the " chapel " on the first floor is a noteworthy canopied seat.   Parts of the west range of the cloister buildings are occupied as a private house.   The successive researches of Harrod, Sir William St. J. Hope, and Dr. Fairweather (see Ingleby, *Supplement*) have left little to be ascertained respecting the plan of this very interesting house.

A little farther on is *West Acre*, where the remains of an Austin priory near the river are not large.   They have recently been explored. Near it is *South Acre*, with brasses and a wooden effigy and screen. And we may as well extend our round to Swaffham, and pick up such places as lie between it and East Dereham.

Swaffham Church is important, with fine tower, aisles, and transepts, and an angel-roof.   In the chancel is the monument and effigy of John Botewright, Master of Corpus Christi College, Cambridge. On this tomb Blomefield saw the names of the angels, Michael and Oriel (for Uriel), the latter a great rarity in England, but apparently mentioned also in Botewright's will.   The angels were at his head, and there was a devil at his feet, all gone.   Gone too are the screen-paintings and the glass representing benefactors which used to be in the north clerestory and aisle.   There remains the Pedlar's seat, a prayer desk made up with the figures of John Chapman and his wife, who built the north aisle, and a pedlar with his dog.   The story of

OXBURGH HALL

the Pedlar of Swaffham is a localized piece of folklore ; it is a tale told in many countries. The pedlar dreamt that if he went to (London Bridge in this case) he would hear of something to his advantage. He went, and wandered up and down for some time. At last a man accosted him and said he seemed to be looking for something. The pedlar told his dream. " If I paid any attention to my dreams," said the other, " I should have to go off to some place called Swaffham and dig under a pear-tree in some orchard [the place was described], for I've dreamt there's a chest of money lying there. But I don't hold with such things." The sequel is easily guessed : the pedlar made his fortune, and built Swaffham aisle. The story is told more accurately and discussed by Sir L. Gomme in *Folklore as an Historic Science*.

On or near the line and road between Swaffham and Dereham is *Necton*, very handsome, with a beautiful roof, early brasses, and gallery and pulpit of the seventeenth century. The roof has angels and apostles : six with Christ are on the north, six on the south with the Virgin ; also four other saints, bishops. These figures stand on brackets. Next, *Sporle*, which has a very large wall-painting of the life of St. Katherine in four rows of seven subjects. In the first row St. Katherine appears before the Emperor and Empress, enters the idol temple, harangues the Emperor ; the idol falls, and Katherine is arrested. In the second row she is in prison, converts the Empress, and the philosopher Porphyrius : is scourged, the wheels are destroyed : the Empress is condemned. In the third the Empress is beheaded and buried by Porphyrius, and he and others are sentenced and executed. In the fourth Katherine is sentenced, beheaded, and buried by angels on Mount Sinai. The last scene is of pilgrims at her shrine.

At *Great Fransham* is a good brass. At *Wendling* rather scanty remains (part of the west end of the church) of a Premonstratensian abbey (a plan is in *Norf. Archæol. Soc.*, vol. v). *Scarning*, long the home of Dr. Augustus Jessopp, has a fine screen. At *Shipdham*, some way south, is a remarkable wooden lectern, and there *was* an old library over the porch.

The above places can be worked from Dereham or Swaffham. But Swaffham must be taken as starting-place for two districts : one south-westerly extending to Downham Market, the other north-westerly extending to Lynn. From Swaffham, which stands almost 250 ft. up,

we dip down into a region where the levels range about 50 ft. and
gradually merge into fen.

On the Brandon road due south *Gt. Cressingham* has a fifteenth-
century manor-house. On the south-west road there is more, viz.
Gooderstone, where the rood-screen has some curious brackets on it,
and the Apostles and Doctors with Angels above them. And then
Oxburgh, where is the very remarkable castellated brick house of the
Bedingfelds (not shown). The house is moated, and three sides of
the court remain, the fourth, in which was the great hall, having been

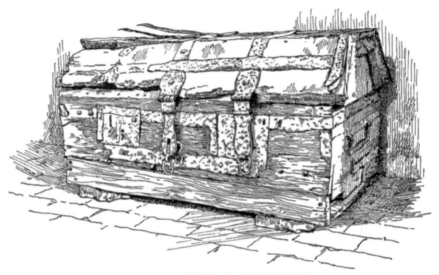

OXBURGH: CHEST IN SOUTH AISLE

pulled down in 1778. It is of the last years of the fifteenth century,
and generally speaking resembles Queens' College, Cambridge. The
great gate-tower is very impressive. The church has a Bedingfeld
tomb of Queen Mary's time, and a screen on which are Etheldreda,
Mary Magdalene, one doubtful saint, St. Thomas of Canterbury,
John Baptist, and Withburga. The sedilia have a cornice of angels.
In Blomefield's time there was a great deal of glass here : the east
window of the north aisle he describes at some length, but evidently
did not understand : it obviously represented the angel appearing to

OXBURGH CHURCH: SCREEN TO THE BEDINGFELD CHAPEL

Joachim, the father of the Virgin, and the Birth of the Virgin. Prophets were in a south-east window, the Nine Orders in the east, with the Nativity, etc., and Apostles with the Creed in the chancel windows.

Beyond *Stoke Ferry* is *Wereham*, in which was the priory of St. Winwaloc. There are remains of it in a farm. Winwaloc is a Breton saint of the fifth to sixth centuries, founder of the famous Abbey of Landevennec. His day is 3rd March, on which there was a great fair at Downham Market : and, as is thought because of the rough weather then to be expected, the rhyme was made, and is still remembered :

> First comes David, then comes Chad,
> Then comes Winnol, roaring like mad.

I have also heard :

> Then comes Winnol's fair, and all the world's mad.

The *Beauties of England and Wales* describe a building at Wereham, known as Winwal House, which they affirm to be of Norman date— a two-storied house with vaulted undercroft, the whole of small dimensions and seemingly complete (33 ft. by 27 by 16). Is it still there ? I do not find it in the books on domestic architecture, and I have not been to Wereham myself.

Next to it is *West Dereham*, site of a Premonstratensian house founded by Hubert Walter in 1188. Here again the *Beauties* expatiate on the fine gatehouse of the abbey with octagonal towers at the angles, and tell how in 1697 Sir Thomas Dereham built wings to it with stately apartments. Now there seems to be nothing but the remains of a large barn and possibly part of the abbot's lodging. The site of the church and cloister is not distinguishable. The parish church has Norman work and a little glass. The Norman font at *Fincham* was engraved over 100 years ago for *Archæologia*. *Barton Bendish* has two churches, each with some Norman work. St. Mary's (*al.*, St. Andrew's) has remains of wall-painting. *Beechamwell* also had a plurality of churches. In the surviving one are early brasses, and the round tower is early. At *Stradsett* is a window of foreign glass of the sixteenth century.

Downham Market and a few parishes round it stand on a patch of higher ground. Then west of Downham we are in the Bedford Level. *Denver* is famous for its sluice, and was the home of a rather forgotten

13

BEAUPRÉ HALL, OUTWELL.

historian of England, Brady, Master of Caius College (*d.* 1700). Westward of this, on the very borders of Cambridgeshire, and indeed partly in it, are some three or four places which have fine churches. *Outwell* and *Upwell* practically join, and constitute " the longest village in England." In Outwell is the romantic and beautiful fragment—with a gatehouse, and some fine heraldic glass—of Beaupré Hall. In the church are good roofs and screen. There was also a great deal of glass and, especially in the Fincham and Beaupré chapels, some survives. The former has part of an Adoration of the Magi, the latter some sainted kings, Lawrence, George, Edmund, etc. Blomefield's later continuator Parkin records these and much more, e.g. Ethelbert almost as large as life (is this the king in the Fincham Chapel ?), and in a south window he says " was formerly this antique piece of painting. A matron in white robe and blue mantle on her knees between four men ; at her feet a fox hanging on a tree wounded in the neck with two arrows, behind and before two monkies with bows shooting at the fox."

Upwell Church is an equally important building, but has not retained so much of its old fittings, having undergone lavish restoration between 1836 and 1842. The roofs are fine. A screen which had unusual paintings on it (recorded by Parkin) has gone. Among the subjects were the Bearing of the Cross, Ascension, Pentecost, and the Trinity.

Emneth is the last church to be noticed in this section. It is very stately, and has Norman and Early English work in the chancel. The roof has figures of our Lord, the Apostles, Michael, and Edmund (the patron) ; angels above these hold the utensils of the Mass. Among remains of glass are St. Citha, the Annunciation, and St. Edmund. The weathercock is said to be as old as the fifteenth century.

The next stage is from Swaffham to *King's Lynn.* But if we went from Downham to Lynn or diverted some way west of the Swaffham–Lynn road, we should pick up two places at which there were small monastic houses, viz. *Marham,* site of a Cistercian nunnery, the only one in the county, and *Shouldham.* Here was a Gilbertine house, of which the barn exists, and various other remains.

The direct Swaffham–Lynn road passes *Narford,* seat of the Fountaines, and *Narborough,* where the Spelmans lived, and their brasses

THE GATEHOUSE, MIDDLETON TOWERS

WALPOLE ST. PETER.

are to be seen. Then *Pentney* with the gatehouse of the Augustinian priory, and *Middleton*. The gatehouse of Lord Scales's castle here is a fine specimen of brick. The church has a screen with the Apostles. *King's Lynn* now lies before us ; and in it there is more to be seen than I can well detail, especially in the way of old merchants' houses, which are apt here to turn a dull brick face on the street, and reserve their real attractions for the inhabitants. But the salient features of the town at least shall be mentioned. The south gate is the only one of the town gates that has been spared. It is of the ordinary type, of the fifteenth century. Near the station is the very curious Red Mount Chapel, visited often by those who were making the Walsingham pilgrimage ; it contained a relic of the Virgin. In plan it is a cross inscribed within an octagon of brick. This cruciform building is vaulted, and access to it is by a double staircase within the octagon, very cleverly planned. The date is 1483, the builder was Robert Corraunce. The details of the stone-work, and particularly the vaulting, of the chapel are excellent. There are two great churches : St. Margaret's has a cathedral-like aspect, for there are two towers at the west end, the southern being mainly fine Early English and the northern Norman at the base. Inside, within the base of the south tower, are the two largest brasses in England, Flemish work of the fourteenth century. Unlike the ordinary type of English brass they are not cut to the shape of the figure, but are in large plates covering the whole stone. One is to Adam de Walsoken (*d.* 1349), the other to Robert Braunche (*d.* 1364). At the base of each is a scene with many figures. Walsoken has a vintage, Braunche a feast with peacocks being brought in. As Mayor he is supposed to have entertained Edward III. These brasses are very difficult to see : they lie close together in a dark place, and the engraving is very delicate ; but rubbings and engravings of them are common enough. Similar brasses are to be found abroad, but not in great numbers, e.g. that of King Eric Menved of Denmark at Ringsted in Seeland, those of two bishops at Lubeck, and that of St. Henry of Finland at Nousis in Finland.

The chancel has a fine thirteenth-century arcade and good lateral screen-work and misericordes. The east window is abnormal, a sort of rose set in a square, high in the wall. The organ case is a good one, and would look better in a gallery (where no doubt it once was).

The instrument was built by Snetzler, and an early organist was Dr. Burney.

The other church, with a modern spire, is the Chapel of St. Nicholas ; in fact, a large fifteenth-century church. It had once fine misericordes, which, at the time of a drastic restoration, made their way to the Architectural Museum in Jermyn Street. Some of the late monuments have epitaphs worth reading.

South Lynn Church has or had panels of Apostles from a screen. A relic of one of the numerous Friars' Houses is the Greyfriars' tower, once the central tower of their church : a very pretty six-sided one, which recalls the pictures of the destroyed central tower of the Black

FROM ST. NICHOLAS' CHURCH, KING'S LYNN :
MISERICORDE—" THRESHING "

Friars (St. Andrew's Hall) at Norwich and the extant one of the Austin Friars at Atherstone. Of secular buildings the Guildhall, near St. Margaret's, contains interesting archives, and the famous fourteenth-century cup with enamelled figures, called King John's. A former college of priests (Thoresby's College), now turned into private houses, is picturesque. But the most pleasing of all is the Dutch-looking Custom House, built in 1683 by Sir William Turner. This is sure to stick in the memory of every visitor to Lynn. One of the mediæval Gildhouses, St. George's Hall, a fifteenth-century brick building, is well seen from the charming bowling-green behind the Globe Hotel, from which place the river also affords a pleasant spectacle. The Museum, called the Greenland Fishery Museum, in

CASTLE RISING: ENTRANCE STAIR

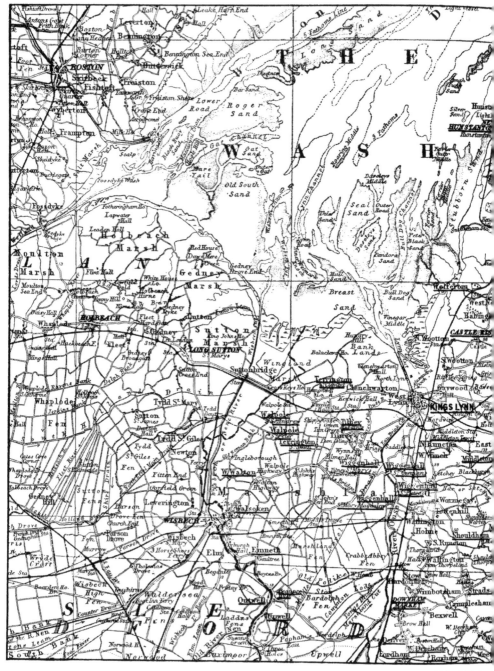

NORFOLK

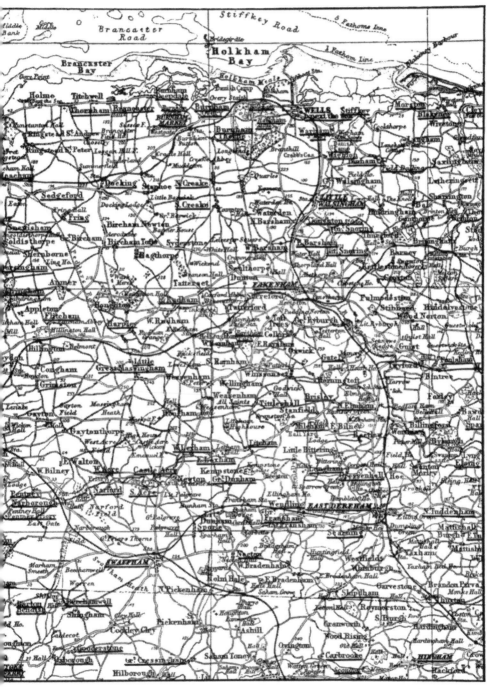

WEST.

Bridge Street, has a good collection of Lynn relics and views, and well deserves a visit.

It will perhaps be best now to take the patch of—

NORTH-WEST NORFOLK

which has been left over, and then return to Lynn and finish with the Marshland churches.

Going northward we come first to *Castle Rising*, where the castle is, next to Norwich Keep, the most important relic of its kind in the county, and has been little interfered with in modern times. It is of the twelfth century. The builder was William d'Albini the Second, late in that century ; we have met with his father before this, as founder of Wymondham priory. The earthworks in which the castle stood are, like those at Castle Acre, thought to be early, some say of Roman date. In the central enclosure were all manner of detached buildings, great hall, kitchens, lodgings, storehouses, etc., and the foundations of a Norman chapel with an apse have been found. But the only building above ground is the great tower (except the fragmentary Norman gatehouse and the fifteenth-century bridge) which is in two stories : the general plan being a square with staircase and vestibule attached to the east side. There was no access to the ground-floor save by winding staircases from the first floor ; this latter was approached by the staircase just mentioned. The fine Norman vestibule at top, with a later vaulted roof, leads into the larger of two rooms which occupy the greater part of the area. Communicating with the smaller one (on the south) is a room called the chapel, the eastern bay of which is vaulted, and has a fourteenth-century east window. There is good Norman arcading on the outside, and some fine Norman windows. The main part of the upper floor is roofless.

In former times our sympathies were asked for Queen Isabella, the She-wolf of France, in that after the death of her beloved Mortimer her son Edward III imprisoned her here for over twenty years till her death in 1350. But it now appears that during those years she travelled to and lived in many parts of England, and died at Hertford Castle. In Henry VIII's time the castle was granted to the Howards, and in the Howard family it has remained.

> " Rising was a seaport town when Lynn was but a marsh,
> Now Lynn it is a seaport town and Rising fares the worse,"

CASTLE RISING CHURCH: WEST FRONT

and till the first Reform Bill it returned two members : its corporation was abolished in 1835.

The church consists of aisleless nave, central tower, south transept, and chancel (modern porch). In the main it is Norman, with an elaborate west front, rich with arcading, but all much restored. In a niche or recess north of the chancel arch a wall-painting of the Crucifixion (13th cent.) is or was visible. The tower has a western arch of horseshoe form and an eastern one pointed. Early English windows have replaced the Norman ones in the chancel. The three lancets which form the east window are deeply splayed inside the church, and have slender shafts, and dog-tooth ornament in the arches. An unfortunate mistake was made when the architect Salvin replaced the battlemented top of the tower (which very likely was a late appendage) by an exotic-looking saddle-backed roof. But the building is beautiful and uncommon.

Next door to the churchyard is the Trinity Hospital or Bede House for twelve women of the neighbourhood, founded by Henry Howard, Earl of Northampton, in 1614. The almswomen, who are presided over by a " governess," live under rules which prescribe the wearing of red cloaks with the badge of the Howards, and high peaked hats. East of our road lie *Flitcham*, with remains of an Augustinian priory, *Harpley*, and the two Massinghams. At *Harpley* the screen has been repainted. I have not seen it, but it is reported to have St. Lawrence, the Virgin and Child, Joachim, Anne and the Virgin, and a series of Prophets.

Coming back to the northern road we are in a pleasant airy region : many kindly royal associations centre round *Sandringham*. *Wolferton*, its station, has a church worth seeing, with the remains of a fine hammer-beam roof, having canopied figures of saints, and some remains of wall-paintings (not in Keyser's book). The churches of *Dersingham*, and still more *Snettisham*, are fine. The west front of the latter recalls the arrangement at Peterborough, and the west window (14th cent.) is magnificent. *Fring*, to the east, has wall-paintings : a St. Christopher on the north wall on a ground semé with five-petalled red flowers ; in the south-east corner a single figure on a blue ground, seemingly a virgin martyr holding a palm or a hook— if the latter, St. Faith. On the east wall the remains of an Annunciation, as I thought. At *Sedgeford* a St. Christopher is very faintly

WEST WALTON CHURCH: SOUTH PORCH.

visible : it was asserted that the Child had three heads symbolizing the Trinity. The appearance was probably due to repainting. A fragment of lettering (*Et in Ihesum*) shows that there was in the windows a series of Apostles with the clauses of the Creed. *Docking,* due east, has a very handsome church. The font is notable—not of the Seven Sacraments type, but having figures of saints round both the bowl and the base. On the base are certainly SS. Katherine, Margaret, Apollonia, and three holding children. There are male saints round the bowl, and of none of these can I be quite certain.

Heacham, a pleasant place, has a fine large church with central tower, but it has been very severely restored. *Hunstanton* is one of the well-known seaside places ; Old Hunstanton has its fairly noteworthy church, with screen, and its fine old Hall (not shown to the public).

We now curve round, following the coast eastward, and come to *Thornham.* Here wall-paintings which I remember (in 1899) have been whitewashed over. Over a door on the south was a man in the stocks, obviously part of the Works of Mercy. The lower panels of the screen have prophets and SS. Paul, Barbara, Mary Magdalene, and, a unique figure, *Lazarus,* with the inscription *Per me multi crediderunt in Ihesum.* The tower is a torso ; the porch and the seating are noteworthy.

Then we pass to *Brancaster,* famous now for golf, in ancient days a great Roman fort, of which little can now be seen. It was called Branodunum. " Near this camp " (I quote the *Beauties of England and Wales*) " was erected by a merchant of Burnham an immense building for malting barley. . . . The length is 312 ft. by 31 in breadth ; and during the season 420 quarters of barley have been wetted weekly." If I mistake not, the malting house is as little visible as the camp.

The group of the *Burnhams* borders on Holkham, and ends our progress eastward. *Burnham Deepdale* is the first. Its Norman font with a series of the twelve months upon it is famous among English fonts.

Next is *Burnham Norton.* It had a house of White Friars, of which a restored gatehouse exists. In the parish church are screen panels much scraped. On these are a donors' inscription for William Croom and his wife Katherine, and there is room at each end for a kneeling effigy. Then we have St. Ethelbert with part of a verse : *Ethelberti mereamur celica . . . ;* a bishop, another called St. Gregory,

and the rest (said to include the Virgin) are very illegible. The
pulpit given by John and Katherine Goldale has the Four Doctors.
Burnham Overy has or had a St. Christopher. *Burnham Market* has a
new and perhaps unique feature in the sculptures on its church tower.
On the *south* face I read St. Francis receiving the stigmata (two
panels). On the *north* God and Moses (?), some Apostles, Adam

BURNHAM DEEPDALE : FONT

and Eve, the beheading of John Baptist. *West :* Herod's feast with
Salome dancing, and Salome with the head ; Peter, Andrew, John,
James, the Martyrdom of St. Thomas of Canterbury. *East :* the
Annunciation, Visitation, Flight into Egypt, Incredulity of Thomas.
Part of the south face remained uncertain.

Burnham Thorpe, birthplace of Nelson, has some mementoes of him
in the church. Between this and North Creake (to the south) are

the fairly considerable ruins of Creake Abbey (Augustinian), including great part of the arcade of the choir.

The two Creakes, North and South, are the last places we visit in this district. *North Creake* has a fine hammer-beam roof and some unusual painted panels, now worked up in the organ case : *Fortitudo* embracing a tower; *Temperancie* pouring water from a jug into a basin ; (name gone) St. Veronica turbaned, holding the vernicle (one would have expected Prudence here) ; Justice with sword, and globe on which scales are painted. At *South Creake* the font was of the Seven Sacraments type, with the Crucifixion, but the reliefs have been very much mutilated. North of the chancel arch is a two-light squint, glazed ; the wall over it is painted with *Ihc* in red. The sedilia are curious ; originally of the thirteenth century, the shafts have been cut away, and the lower face of the sill of a Perpendicular window above has been carved with demi-angels holding tilting shields, alternating with large paterae. There is some glass in several windows. At the east end of the north aisle some lettering belonging to the Creed ; a four-teenth-century Angel with censer ; a saint-figure with the head of a Christ crowned with thorns, from a Crucifixion. In the same aisle a window with a Trinity in the tracery, and six figures, four of Apostles with Creed-scrolls, and two of Angels. The canopies have seated lions in gold. Towards south-west a window with a small Crucifixion and four feathered angels, and two saints, Helena (?) with tau-cross, and Agatha, or Apollonia, with pincers. A western window has a head of Christ, a seated headless figure, a six-winged seraph or cherub standing on a wheel, and fragments of another, and an Apostle with a Creed-scroll—*Ascendit ad celos.* All of this is of the fourteenth century.

The last fragment of Norfolk is that which lies west of Lynn, and contains the magnificent—

MARSHLAND CHURCHES

or rather the northern and more important group of them, those to the south having been already noticed.

Nearest to the Cambridgeshire border, and practically a suburb of Wisbech, is *Walsoken*, which has the finest Norman nave and chancel of any parish church in Norfolk. Aisles (14th cent.) and a fifteenth-century clerestory have been added, and a spire to the fine western

WEST WALTON : TOWER

tower. The roof has coloured figures on the helves. There are six-teen of these, and most are Apostles. A large figure is over the western arch. The font has the Seven Sacraments and Crucifixion on the bowl and saints round the inscribed base, of whom these are dis-tinguishable : Magdalene, Stephen, Mary, and Paul, Katherine, Peter, Dorothy. There is also a good piece of screen-work, and some extremely fine bench-ends.

West Walton is not less remarkable than Walsoken as an example of the very best thirteenth-century work. Its tower, very massive Early English, with large window openings, stands apart. In the church it is difficult to know what to praise most : the western door, with double arch, inside a magnificently moulded outer arch ; the windows (e.g. at south-east), though many have been replaced by poor Perpendicular ones ; the really splendid arcade between nave and aisles, with detached Purbeck shafts. All are exceptionally beautiful. There is little in the way of imagery : the scutcheons of the Twelve Tribes (17th cent.) are painted in medallions between the arches, and there is an epigram on a board commemorative of great floods in 1613, 1614, and 1670.

> Aethiopem dicas Numen laterem ve lavasse
> Heu post tot fluctus sordida culpa manet.
> Surely our Sins were tinctured in grain,
> May we not say the Labour was in vain,
> Soe many washings, still the spotts remain.

Walpole St. Andrew is less notable ; but it has a picture (Italian, of the Entombment) and what is thought to be an anchorite's cell in one of the buttresses of the tower.

Walpole St. Peter, however, is reckoned by some to be the finest of all these churches. It is indeed very stately Perpendicular. Outside, we note the large porch, the turrets on the east wall of the nave, and the arched passage beneath the chancel. Inside, the Jacobean screen crossing the church, the font cover of like date with charming pilasters and patterned panels ; some good seating. The chancel has five canopied niches on either side, and there must have been a great display of glass in its large windows. Screen panels remain with figures of (north) Katherine, Virgin and Child, Margaret, John

14

Evangelist, James the Great, Thomas (south), Peter, Paul, Andrew, Magdalene, Dorothy, Barbara.

There are traces of wall-paintings on the south of the chancel arch, and a king's head beside an altar on the north, in a niche. But there was a great deal more when Parkin made his inspection. It is some time since I recorded any of these lost glories, so here, near the end of my survey, I will indulge myself.

In the east window of the south aisle was Sir Thomas Daniel kneeling and invoking St. James (*Tu sis memor mei Jacobe in presentia dei*).

In one of the upper windows (south aisle) " a profane presentation of the Supreme Being habited in a loose purple gown with a long beard, resting His right hand on a staff of gold and crowned with glory ; pointing out the forefinger of His left hand as dictating to the Virgin Mary, who is seated before Him, with a pen in her hand and paper on a desk before her. The Deity stands at the door or entrance of a castle embattled and with turrets, surrounded by a wall embattled ; within this wall is the Virgin, and many angels are looking down from the tower, etc. There has been a legend, and the word *Convertit* is now legible. The artist has represented a great degree of majesty in the face of the Deity, and seems, like Phidias of old, to have had those verses of Homer in his thoughts : ' ἦ, καὶ κυανέῃσιν,' etc."

WALPOLE ST. PETER : DETAIL OF STALL

What this subject can have been I do not see.

There were also (as at West Walton) the shields of the tribes on the nave walls ; paintings of the Virgin and Child and St. John ; many saints in the north aisle windows, and arms and effigies of Rochfords.

The chancel windows had glass
of 1423-5. In the south were
Alban, William of York, Hugh of
Lincoln, Withburga, Etheldreda,
Sexburga. On the north : John
Evangelist, John of Beverley,
Edmund of Canterbury survived,
besides donative inscriptions.
The *Terringtons* are the most
northerly of this group. *Terrington
St. John* has a so-called Priests'
House attached to the tower, much
as at Walpole St. Andrew and
Tilney All Saints. *Terrington St.
Clement* is another competitor for the
first place among these churches :
very spacious, cruciform in plan,
with splendid turrets at the west
end, and a detached tower at the
north-west. The south porch is
large and fine. The whole building
is Perpendicular. Between the
windows of the nave clerestory are
canopied niches, and over the west
arch of the crossing are seven more;
over the east arch (or chancel arch)
is a window. The font cover is very
interesting, the upper or spire-part
mediæval, the lowest story changed
to Jacobean with classical pillars.
It opens, and within are seventeenth-century paintings of the
Evangelists, the Baptism of Christ,
and the Temptation. The Baptism
is accompanied by the verse : *Voce
Pater, Natus corpore, Flamen ave—
Mat.* 3 (i.e. at the Baptism the
Father was manifested by the

TERRINGTON ST. CLEMENT :
ST. CHRISTOPHER

WIGGENHALL ST. MARY THE VIRGIN :
DETAIL OF BENCH—ST. LEONARD

Voice, the Son by His bodily presence, the Spirit by the Dove).

Returning southward we come to the *Tilneys*, of which only *Tilney All Saints* asks for attention. The nave arcade is for the most part Norman ; a fifteenth-century clerestory and hammer-beam roof have been added. The chancel has side-chapels, and the screens to these are mediæval, but the main screen Jacobean. The "anchorites' house," if such it is, has been mentioned. A fair amount of glass is recorded here by Parkin-Blomefield, mostly Apostles and single figures of other saints ; in the north chapel was a scene of Confession, perhaps from a Seven Sacraments window.

The tomb of the giant-killer Hickathrift was once shown in the churchyard of one of the Tilneys ; I am not sure which.

The *Wiggenhalls* follow. There are four : *St. Mary, St. Mary Magdalene, St. Peter, St. German.*

At *St. Mary* the old seats are pronounced by Dr. Cox to be "the finest in the country, almost perfect in their original fifteenth - century condition." They have open-work backs, popeys with flanking figures in the round, and saints in high relief under canopies on the ends. I regret that I have no list of these saints to offer : there are others at Walsoken.

The screen panels have eight saints (Virgin and Child, John Baptist, Magdalene, Barbara, M a r g a r e t, "Scholastica," Katherine, Dorothy). The brass eagle is old (1518) ; there is a good tomb with effigies.

At *St. Mary Magdalene*, which is also a fine building, there is a long series of small figures of saints in the tracery lights of the windows of the north aisle. They have their names, and many of them are extremely uncommon. They seem to have been the gift of Isabel of Ingoldsthorp in 1470. The system on which they are arranged is not obvious. Nelson records (beginning from the west : I. SS. Calixtus, Hilary, Brice, Aldhelm, Sixtus, Sampson, Germanus, Cuthbert. In the next window are such unusual figures as Hippolytus ... Januarius, P r o s d o c i m u s (Apostle of Padua), Romanus (of Rouen), and so forth. The order is not that of the Calendar. The screen is recorded to have had the Evangelistic emblems and St. Agatha.

WIGGENHALL ST. GERMANS : DETAIL OF BENCH—THE FOURTH OF THE " DEADLY SINS "

At *St. Germans* is more seating (a good deal restored) of the type of that at St. Mary.

If I end my survey of Norfolk here, I am under no illusions as to

its completeness. I may have given some notice of between 200 and
300 buildings ; and though it is *probably* the case that none of great
importance have been passed over without a word, many of those I
have mentioned deserve more words, and scores of others that I have
not mentioned contain some feature which many a traveller will find
extremely interesting.   It is almost always worth while to halt and
look into a Norfolk church.

   I have been very relentless in cataloguing saints on screens and
such things, but I have comforted myself with the reflection that he
who makes the tour of Norfolk and is not prepared to interest himself
in these details might just as well stop at home and save his time
and money.

ARMS OF THE SEE OF NORWICH

THE APOSTLES IN ART

PERHAPS after seeing the Apostles painted and carved again and again on the screens and roofs and in the windows of the churches I have been describing, the tourist may like to be told, without the trouble of referring to the many other books in which the information is given, why the attributes assigned to each of them are so assigned, and what they mean.

The answer is that they are derived either from what is told about each Apostle in the New Testament, or from the legendary lives of them which were made up in early times.

Very few authentic traditions about the Twelve Apostles and St. Paul were preserved. It was not even clearly remembered where most of them had preached the gospel, or where and how they had died. Herod beheaded James the brother of John, that is certain. I do not think it less certain that Peter and Paul suffered martyrdom at Rome, and personally I believe that John died at Ephesus in extreme old age ; though many would tell you that this was not John the Apostle, but another John, the Presbyter. But this accounts for only four out of thirteen. More information had to be supplied, both about these four and the rest of the band. Let us see how it came and of what sort it was.

About the middle of the second century someone wrote what he called the *Acts of John* : professedly he was a disciple of the Apostle, but his book is a romance, and had for its object the popularizing of a particular sort of doctrine—it does not matter exactly what, but doctrine of an heretical kind. Shortly after this another man, a priest in Asia, composed some *Acts of Paul*, on the model of those of John. Next, a generation later, the *Acts of Peter* were written, and at intervals after that, those of *Thomas and Andrew*—five very long romances, full of exciting miracles, and not very exciting discourses. Then there was an interval ; after which perhaps in the fourth century another outburst of activity came on. In this it seems that the monks of Egypt were the protagonists. The romances became much more sensational, and the doctrine less so. Between the fourth century and the sixth each of the Apostles is supplied with a legend to himself. It is from these romances, commonly called the Apocryphal Acts of the Apostles, that most of the attributes they carry are ultimately derived, as I have said ; but the romances had been severely abridged before they got within the ken of the artists. Particularly was this the case with the unorthodox Acts. From these the heretical prayers and discourses were purged away, and only the narratives left ; the story of the martyrdom or death of the Apostle being often preserved apart from the rest, to be read as Lessons on his feast-day.

This being premised, I will go through the list of the Apostles and comment briefly on the attribute of each :

Peter's is Biblical : he carries the keys of the Kingdom of Heaven.

Paul's is the sword of his martyrdom.

These two are found at an earlier date than the rest of the attributes ; for it is perhaps not till the fourteenth century that we find each Apostle provided with such a thing. In early representations they carry palms or crosses and books.

John has the cup and a serpent or dragon proceeding out of it, which dragon represents the poison leaving the cup when John blessed it. He was made to drink poison, of which the virulence had already been tested on two condemned criminals. We see, in windows of the thirteenth century in France, how the poison was made, by pounding up snakes and toads in a mortar. After a prayer, in which he asked that all the venom might be made harmless, John drank the cup ; and thereafter made the still incredulous heathen priest Aristodemus cast his garment upon the dead criminals, and thereby raise them to life.

Andrew has the saltire cross. There is nothing in his Acts to show that the cross on which he suffered was of unusual form, but, perhaps to differentiate him from our Lord and St. Peter, he is shown in thirteenth-century pictures as crucified horizontally ; and from this to the saltire was a short step.

James the Great appears as a pilgrim with staff and scallop shell. Here is a symbol of different origin. The pilgrimage to St. James of Compostella was one of the most popular in Europe, and the thought of it was the first that would occur to anyone in connexion with the name of this Apostle. So he is seen really as a pilgrim to his own shrine.

James the Less has a club. This Apostle, of whom nothing is known, was in the Latin Church identified or at least confused with James the brother of the Lord and first bishop of Jerusalem. (The Greek Church does not make this mistake.) The earliest of Church historians, Hegesippus, told a story of this James being cast down from the Temple by the Jews, and killed with a fuller's bat or club. Hence the symbol.

Thomas has a lance, in accordance with his Acts, which tell of his missionary career in India, and of his being pierced by four soldiers with lances.

Philip has either a long cross (he was crucified at Hierapolis according to his Acts), or, as on most of the screens in East Anglia, three loaves. This derives from John vi. and the share he takes in the feeding of the five thousand.

Matthew as Apostle has a halbert : a little obscure, this, for the Acts which the artists followed only tell how he was stabbed while ministering at the altar. As Evangelist his attribute is well known to be the Angel (more correctly the winged man).

Bartholomew holds the knife with which he was flayed. The flaying is a very late tradition (?13th cent.), but took the fancy of artists. The horrid representation in Michelangelo's *Last Judgment* of the Apostle bearing his skin may be remembered, or the still worse one in Milan Cathedral—the statue by Marco Agrati.

Simon and *Jude* are more difficult. Their Acts tell us how they preached in Persia, and were finally slain in a riot in a heathen temple. And other floating traditions say that Simon was crucified and Jude shot with arrows, or, if Jude is identified with Thaddaeus (as often), that he died a natural death. The artists do not follow these stories. On our screens we see Simon with a fish and Jude with a boat—the latter as a fisherman, the former too, perhaps, or else as having taken part in the miracle of feeding, like Philip. Elsewhere I do not think Jude has any fixed attribute ; but Simon I have seen carrying a scimitar (which does agree with the Acts), and much oftener, in late pictures, a saw, for which no evidence whatever can be produced.

Matthias is apt to carry a halbert, like Matthew, and doubtless he was confused with Matthew in the minds of the artists, as he was in the legends, where it is very difficult sometimes to tell which of the two is meant. There are no proper ancient Acts of Matthias. None were attempted till perhaps the twelfth century, when a monk of an abbey at Trèves, which boasted the possession of Matthias' body, wrote some, professing to take them from an old Hebrew book. According to these, the Apostle was stoned and beheaded.

The figures of Apostles which I have been discussing so far are those which we see painted on screens or carved on roofs. In the relics of painted windows we find a somewhat different treatment, namely, when each Apostle bears a sentence from the Creed. A legend grew up (how early I do not know, but it was being used in the twelfth century) that after Pentecost the Apostles composed the Creed which goes by their name, each contributing a clause. Peter begins : *Credo in deum Patrem,* and Matthias ends *Et vitam aeternam Amen.* Paul is, of course, excluded from this series : he was not yet a Christian. For purposes of art this conception was very often enriched by the addition of twelve figures of Prophets, each bearing a prophecy corresponding with a clause of the Creed. A typical series would be this :

Peter : Credo in deum Patrem Omnipotentem creatorem caeli et terrae.

Andrew : Et in Ihesum Christum, filium eius unicum dominum nostrum.

James : Qui conceptus est de spiritu sancto, natus ex Maria virgine.

John : Passus sub Pontio Pilato, crucifixus, mortuus et sepultus.

Thomas : Descendit ad inferna, tertia die resurrexit a mortuis.

James the Less : Ascendit ad caelos, sedet ad dexteram dei patris omnipotentis.

Philip : Inde uenturus est iudicare uiuos et mortuos.

Bartholomew : Credo in spiritum sanctum.

Jeremiah : Patrem inuocabunt me qui feci caelum et terram.

David : Dominus dixit ad me Filius meus es tu.

Isaiah : Ecce virgo concipiet et pariet filium.

Zechariah : Aspicient omnes ad me quem confixerunt.

Hosea : O mors ero mors tua, morsus tuus ero inferne.

Amos : Qui aedificat in caelo ascensionem suam.

Malachi : Accedam ad uos in iudicio et ero testis uelox.

Joel : Effundam de spiritu meo super omnem carnem.

Matthew : Sanctam ecclesiam catholicam, sanctorum communionem.

Simon : Remissionem peccatorum.

Jude : Carnis resurrectionem.

Matthias : Et vitam aeternam. Amen.

Obadiah : Inuocabunt omnes nomen domini et seruient ei.

Micah : Deponet omnes iniquitates uestras.

Ezekiel : Educam uos de sepulcris uestris.

Daniel : Euigilabunt omnes, alii ad uitam alii ad opprobrium.

But there are plenty of variations in the choice of the prophecies, though the division of the Creed among the Apostles is fairly well fixed.

INDEX

27499477R00173

Printed in Great Britain
by Amazon